John Webb is an ordinary person, with a sense of adventure, whose father was struck down with Alzheimer's disease. It led John to find out more about this killing disease, opened up his eyes to conditions in one particular Care Home and he took up the challenge to hopefully climb to the roof of Africa to raise money for Alzheimer's research.

To Carl & Family

All the Best

John (SJ)

Dedicated to the memory of my late father William and to my wife Susan. Without both of these people in my life, the trek, the memories and this book would never have happened.

John Webb

EVERY STEP OF THE WAY

AUSTIN MACAULEY PUBLISHERS™

LONDON • CAMBRIDGE • NEW YORK • SHARJAH

A CIP catalogue record for this title is available from the British Library.

ISBN 9781398493674 (Paperback)
ISBN 9781398493681 (ePub e-book)

www.austinmacauley.co.uk

First Published 2024
Austin Macauley Publishers Ltd®
1 Canada Square
Canary Wharf
London
E14 5AA

Special thanks to…

Andrew… you made the impossible possible.

Mother-in-law, **Marie**, who quietly gave so much in many ways.

Keith and **Sue**, for your help and interest.

The people of the Village, particularly for the help given on the cricket day and the auction.

Friends **Aileen** and **Clive**, great supporters, particularly to Susan.

My late mother, **Doris** (RIP).

The late **Steve P** (RIP).

The late **Stuart P** (RIP).

To **Andy** for the loan of the field for cricket and to **Alun** for the loan of your field for fireworks.

And to **all those** not mentioned who messaged and supported. To…

Susan, my wife, without your idea, unwavering support, encouragement, selflessness and love, this never would have happened.

Preface

If you want a happy ending that depends, of course, on where you stop your story. – Orson Welles

When friends and family found out I was writing this book, the immediate question was, why did it take you so long?

The answer is quite simple. Who would really be interested in reading about an "older" bloke walking up a mountain and additionally, how on earth can I find 40,000 to 50,000 words describing the events of that week in September 2008 and the previous 12 months, whether it was successful or not?

For example, man tries to get fit as he can, given his age and history, man walks up mountain, does he get to the top? Man walks down mountain. Man goes on holiday. Not actually inspiring stuff and could be completed in a couple of chapters, at most.

I had, in fact, given some thought, on and off, to putting it down in writing for quite a while but other commitments in life distracted me and it was only ever just a thought but a thought that never really left me.

Until, that is, I got to thinking of it more deeply. The more I thought the more I was convinced it wasn't just about an attempt to climb the highest point of Africa, but the reasons for doing it were so integral. I wondered just how deep a topic it could be.

Where would it lead me? To what areas would it pull me?

Alzheimer's disease itself is far more than just a book that I could ever write. It is a complicated minefield of questions and some answers, of discoveries and disappointments, of research and gaining knowledge. I am no expert in these matters but through experience I have learned a lot more than I knew prior to 2001. How it takes people, how they behave, how cruel it is, what care is required and how it strips the dignity of those struck down by it.

So, there was one important topic that maybe I needed to look into, to get a deeper meaning of why I wanted to write this book and also to perhaps discover, why many people are affected by Alzheimer's and other types of dementia, as well as my possible future relationship with this illness.

Then there is my father. In many ways an unremarkable man leading an unremarkable life but delving into his history, took me on another voyage of discovery. I already knew about him, obviously, but other things came out during his illness and digging a little deeper into his life led me to perhaps understand him a little more, as we didn't always have a harmonious interaction together.

Both subjects, being, Alzheimer's and my father, then pushed me into the dark area of levels of care in care homes or in one home in particular, which I am sure is not unique. Here was something that not only needed research but crying out to be exposed without laying oneself open to any libellous action. The only way to discover if the poor treatment of patients in these homes, apart from my own experience, is to get the views of opinions of relatives of those people who are or have been resident in one of these facilities.

Another topic for me to look into, and it was important to me personally, was smoking and more importantly, after getting hooked on it, giving it up, which I know many, many people find difficult to do. I needed to research this for my own benefit, as the decision I had taken two years earlier would play a part in whether I was convinced I could be successful or not in completing this challenge.

Finally, I needed to delve some way into lumbar decompression surgery, as a result of self-inflicted damage I had participated in. On the face of it, not the most riveting of subjects but quite important nonetheless. Again, here was an area that played a big part in my decision to undertake this adventure, whether it would hamper my training and ultimately my success, or failure.

So, putting everything together, with excitement and curiosity as to where it could lead me, I embarked upon researching and writing this book with the hope that I can fashion it into, not just a good read but that I am able to, maybe, provide some answers and ask more questions for people who have been, or are, or will be, affected by the things I touch on.

If readers can relate to the subject matter, I will be happy. If people can say it retained their interest, I will be delighted. If anybody can find inspiration from any of the topics I have looked into, that will help them cope better or make more sense of their personal situation, it will all have been worthwhile. Ultimately, if it encourages anybody to undertake an extreme fund-raising challenge for any worthy cause I would love to know, and maybe I am able to lend support in one way or another.

In my own inexperienced way, I have attempted to shine a light on these different, but related areas, certainly for me. Additionally, there are those who also have been, or currently are, or will be in the future, touched by them. It is likely that this will be a vast number of people within the United Kingdom. My attempted climb of Kilimanjaro is without doubt on the periphery in comparison to such important things but remains the catalyst for bringing it all together.

I have, throughout this book, tried to stay away from typical clichés like "my journey" as it is quite obvious it is a journey but it is more of a challenge, an adventure and was, without any shadow of a doubt, the most exciting time of my life.

SJ

Prologue

Every accomplishment starts with the decision to try.
– John F Kennedy

It was midnight on 25 September 2008 and extremely cold. I knew it was going to get even colder in the next few hours. Looking into the blackness ahead the only things visible were a number of torchlights bobbing up and down.

'It's OK John,' a voice from behind me said, 'all we have to do is climb the equivalent of Ben Nevis and we are at the top.'

'As easy as that huh, George,' I joked.

I was standing at the departure point of our final ascent camp on Mount Kilimanjaro, Africa's highest mountain, the highest free-standing mountain in the world, and to complete the climb we had to negotiate the height of the UK's highest mountain, Ben Nevis, at 1,345 metres (4,413 ft.), in the early hours of the morning dealing with minus temperatures and knowing the higher we go the colder it will get and the air will become thinner and thinner and it was no secret that not all of us were going to make it to the summit. Was snow and ice going to make it even more difficult or even prevent us from reaching our goal? We would have to wait and see, even if we managed to get to that height, that is.

Altitude sickness is the main cause of failure in climbing high points and there was no doubt, of our original party of 24, some of whom had already failed in their challenge at this point, more would also suffer and have to be removed from the mountain for their own safety.

George, our leader and guide had done the climb several times before. He knew what to expect he was a professional but I was 57 years old at the time, an ex-smoker, had serious lower back surgery only two years before and had, in fact, only started training for the event 12 months prior to taking on this challenge. I had coped well so far and pleased with how I felt but this last climb was stepping up to another level, literally, but it was going into the unknown for me and I found it exciting, invigorating and was very curious as to how I would cope, with the possibility of failure not in my thinking whatsoever. I certainly wasn't intimidated by what lay ahead, I just wanted to see that sign that told me I had reached the top.

I was the oldest in our party to reach the final ascent. We had three tour guides from UK plus a lady doctor. In addition, we were assigned a local guide. My guide was a really nice man in his 30s, a Tanzanian, called Oscar or Stick as they used to call him due to his height and slimness. Probably 196 centimetres tall or more and like a rake. He was the quiet type who had climbed to the summit numerous times; it was second nature to him.

'John. You're with me,' he said. 'You'll do OK.'

I felt reassured.

This was day five. We had climbed the previous day from morning after breakfast and had arrived in camp at around 4.00 pm. There was just time to change, eat and sleep a while before being woken at 11.00 pm to start our final ascent at 12.00 midnight. Eating as much porridge as possible for energy and drinking copious amounts of water to avoid dehydration, we geared up ready for the final push to the top.

Mount Kilimanjaro stands at 5,895 metres (19,340 ft.) and is the highest point on the continent of Africa. It actually has three peaks or volcanic cones; Shira at 3,962 metres (12,999 ft.), Mawenzi at 5,149 metres (16,893 ft.) and the highest peak is Kibo, although the actual summit is known as Uhuru Peak.

It was reported that a German missionary and explorer, Johannes Rebmann had first seen Kilimanjaro in 1840, a claim that was confirmed by English explorer, Harry Johnston and English geographer, Halford Mackinder. However, this was disputed by Hans Meyer who stated that Rebmann only arrived in Africa in 1846 and, according to Rebmann's diary, saw the mountain on 11 May 1848. It is understood that Rebmann made no attempt to climb it.

The first Europeans to reach the summit were German Geographer, Hans Meyer and Austrian mountaineer, Ludwig Purtcheller in 1889, in what was then German East Africa. Meyer had attempted the climb on two previous occasions. The first attempt in 1887 he had reached the base of Kibo but did not have the right equipment due to deep snow and ice. A second attempt was to be made by Meyer the following year along with cartographer, Oscar Baumann. Having explored the Usambara region in northeastern Tanganyika, as it was then called, their plan was to make their way to Kilimanjaro and attempt to summit. This they could not do due to a revolution taking place called the Abushiri revolt. Led by Abu Bashir ibn Salim al-Harthi or Abushiri for short, a mixture of the Arab and Swahili people caused an insurrection against the granting of certain areas of the coast of East Africa by the Sultan of Zanzibar to the German East Africa Company. Abushiri led the uprising and during this time Meyer and Baumann were arrested and imprisoned by Abushiri's cohorts. They were released on payment of a large ransom and the revolt was supressed by the arrival of a German expeditionary corps. Abushiri himself fled but was betrayed to the Germans and was sentenced to death. He was publicly hanged in the town of Pangani, a historic Swahili settlement, in December 1889.

Hans Meyer had heard of Purtcheller's mountaineering feats in the Alps and invited him to join his party for his third attempt in 1889. They were accompanied by an 18-year-old Tanzanian guide by the name of Yohani Kinyala Lauwo, later called Mzee Lauwo. He was to be the only African in the party but no records show if he or any other African had climbed to the summit before. Climbing through thick snow and ice, Purtcheller cut steps with his ice axe and reached the edge of the crater just 150 metres from the summit. Both were suffering from the effects of the thin air and hard climbing so returned to their camp at 4,300 metres (14,107 ft.). Three days later, feeling well after a good rest, they followed their previous route and were able to continue to the top, becoming the first known people to climb to the highest point in Africa.

It is worth noting that the area was still occupied and influenced by Germany at the outbreak of World War I but on 13 July 1916 the British Naval ship, HMS Severn, bombarded the town for 10 days forcing the surrender of Pangani by Germany to additional British and naval forces.

Kilimanjaro is not thought to have an exact meaning but is closely tied to two words. In Swahili, "Kilima" means mountain and from a local tribe "The Chagga" or "Jagga" the word "Njaro" means whiteness. Put together the meaning is Mountain of Whiteness probably referring to the ever-present snowcap at the top.

The snow has covered Kilimanjaro since the last ice age about 11,000 years ago but it is melting. Estimates show that from 1912 to 1953 the ice reduced by 1.1% each year. From 1953 to 1989 this rose to 1.4% and from 1989 to 2007, the ice reduced by 2.4%. The increases are thought to be due to global climate change and it is estimated at the current rate that the ice will have disappeared by 2033, only 12 years from when I write this. The melting ice is a lifeline for people, vegetation and animals with over 1,000,000 people being directly supported by it. The Chagga people use a series of canals and water diversions to irrigate their farms and the disappearance of the ice cap will be a major catastrophe. Many, many more people will also be affected with the current deforestation on the lower elevations and the disappearance of the rich vegetation on the green slopes could cause a humanitarian crisis.

Mount Kilimanjaro National Park became a UNESCO world heritage site in 1987. World heritage sites exist all over the world but are deemed to be special by UNESCO as they are worthy of preservation for the present and future generations. Regardless of where in the world they are situated they are regarded as being in trust for all the people of the world and protected by international treaty.

Further, a world heritage site brings benefits such as economic regeneration, conservation, education and additional funding as well as increases in tourism which is always a benefit to the local economies. Other heritage sites include The Taj Mahal, The Great Barrier Reef and The Great Wall of China to mention just a few, which demonstrates the importance of Kilimanjaro National Park when mentioned in the same breath as such famous landmarks.

The United Kingdom currently contains 33 world heritage sites.

There are around 154 animal species within Kilimanjaro National Park including bush babies, blue monkeys, chameleons, elephants, rhinos and leopards. We didn't see any of these, I'm happy to say, but we did come into contact with one or two others during the trek that I will mention later.

Chapter 1
William John Webb

For some moments in life there are no words.
– David Seltzer

William John Webb was my father. Nothing particularly notable about that but indirectly he was the cause, or the reason, I was taking on the challenge of attempting to scale Mount Kilimanjaro.

In the winter of 2001, in Liverpool, England, William, or Billy as he was called, or Mad Billy by some and Willy by others, went for a walk to the shops in quite deep snow, to pick up his evening newspaper, The Liverpool Echo. He experienced a fall in the snow and never ever returned to the home he shared with my mother, Doris.

The fall, as it turned out, was not totally because of the snow but he had what appears to have been a TIA (Transient ischaemic attack) or mini stroke for short. He was taken to hospital where, in time, he was diagnosed with Alzheimer's disease. When I first visited him in hospital, he said he knew who I was. I wasn't quite sure but his conversation was strange. He kept imagining that he was on the world-famous docks at Liverpool and that a ship was coming in. He was waiting for it to unload so he could get some of the cargo onto his lorry to transport to any point in the United Kingdom. Most of his working life was spent driving lorries around this island, as well as lorry driving around Europe during World War II, and clearly, although having retired some years earlier, the affect that Alzheimer's had on his brain had taken him back to his working life.

Alzheimer's disease is named after Dr Alois Alzheimer, a German psychiatrist and neurologist who found, in 1906, that a woman had died after suffering severe memory loss and disorientation. He discovered she had degenerative brain disease and so he set out to uncover why this had happened. Even today, causes of Alzheimer's and other forms of dementia are not completely understood and statistics regarding whether there is a genetic link is uncertain. Alzheimer's is the most common form of dementia with more women than men contracting the disease. Symptoms can develop in people as young as 30 years of age and at this time it is estimated that around 850,000 people in the UK are affected with 1 in 14 of the population over the age of 65 being the highest concentration.

There are three main stages to Alzheimer's. Early stage is when people forget conversations and cannot recall names, and trying, at times, to find the correct word in a conversation. Mid Stage shows an increase in confusion, getting lost, delusions and disturbed sleep. Later Stage causes difficulty in swallowing and eating, weight loss and speech and memory loss. There is a tendency to say, certainly when Early Stage is apparent, that it's just old age but these signs should be taken seriously and kept under observation. Something which I unknowingly, at the time, had recognised in my father.

Additionally, certain studies in recent years have attempted to ascertain a link between loss of hearing and Alzheimer's disease and other types of dementia. At this point it is unclear if an individual strains to constantly hear sounds, this brings on dementia, or, hearing loss is a consequence of contracting Alzheimer's. Certainly, there is every reason to investigate further but my father did suffer hearing loss particularly in his left ear for quite a long period of time. However, this was explained by the many years of lorry driving and having the engine right next to him, loud and almost daily, nobody at that time ever gave it a second thought.

Even a hearing specialist he visited diagnosed his loss of hearing was probably due to the engine noise. However, there was never any suggestion that he was suffering from dementia at that point even though very little was known about any connection. Knowledge of Alzheimer's and dementia in general was nowhere near as advanced as it is now but I do recall my grandfather also suffering hearing loss but as a child I put that down to "selective" hearing particularly when my grandmother was around.

As an aside, prior to my mother passing away with various complaints, one of which was vascular dementia, she too was reliant on hearing aids for many years.

The Alzheimer's Society and Alzheimer's Research are, as I understand it, funded partly by our National Health Service and partly relies on donations from the public, be it by direct payments or by sponsorship or by supporting fund raising events, such as my Kilimanjaro trek. Other research charities benefit too but there are so many charities in existence that I wonder if there is not a better way of funding large organisations such as Alzheimer's Society. Apart from Alzheimer's and dementia charities in general, the other major organisation doing wonderful work in research and finding answers is Cancer Research UK. As both charities affect the lives of so many people throughout our islands it occurs to me that both should be government funded not only in research but treatment and care also. It is not just those people struck down directly with these insidious diseases but the affect that has on so many others. Others of a working age whose careers are disrupted, whose incomes are reduced as they have to provide care to loved ones. There is also reliance, in some cases, on younger family members who have their education disrupted because they are providing care for older family members, which cannot be right. State funding removes the pressure from charities to continually raise funds to maintain their life-saving work, and let them concentrate on more important things like actually saving lives. Additionally, smaller charities, of which there are so many, can be the beneficiaries of the generosity of the good people of the United Kingdom.

These are just my opinions based on the knowledge I have gained over the years, seeing relatives and friends suffer and loved ones left to grieve when there could be a better way to deal with the question of funding. I could go on but I won't, much. The National Lottery raises millions of pounds each week for "good causes". Show me a better cause than saving lives, funding meaningful research or the specialist care required by people suffering from this illness!

William John Webb was born in Liverpool on 8 February 1923 to William John Webb (not very original with their names) and Charlotte Webb. He was the oldest son in a family of about 10+ children with one or two dying during the birth and another son Donald passing away at an early age. The number of children was not untypical of families at that time although our family folklore seems to suggest that every time my grandfather saw my grandmother without any clothes on, she fell pregnant!

Academically my dad wasn't the brightest. To a degree he was hampered because he was left-handed which in 1920s and 1930s was not only a disadvantage but also, made him a victim of cruelty by some teachers. One or two would actually tie his left hand behind the back of his chair to force him to write with his right hand. Any attempt to persuade him not to do what was natural to him failed and until his dying day he remained a lefty. In any event, his future had already been carved out for him by his father, regardless of any direction he wanted to venture into in his working life.

He would be, eventually, going lorry driving as my grandfather had been most of his working life. In fact, my grandfather had been the rear driver on a 100-ton lorry, one of only two in the country at the time, transporting items such as railway locomotives and other exceptionally heavy machinery and the like. On leaving school, my father worked for a renowned department store in Liverpool city centre, George Henry Lee. Being too young to drive he was second man, learning the art of delivering goods including furniture and how to manoeuvre it without damaging anything. His experience in this field became useful when various members of the family moved home from time to time in later years.

At the start of World War II he was assigned, on certain nights, to be posted on the roof of the store, on fire watch, in case any incendiary devices were dropped and caused fires and possibly damaging the valuable furniture and other goods in the store below. He was in fact mentioned in glowing terms, as it were, on more than one occasion. My father then got himself a job with a local newspaper and enjoyed his working life there having been told that he had a future there, but Grandad had different ideas and made him resign and go and work for The Liverpool Warehousing Company in Cotton Street, Liverpool just over the Dock Road from the very important dockyards. I don't believe it ever occurred to him to stand up to his father and tell him he wanted to remain in his current employment.

At 19, he was conscripted into the army as a lorry driver, and spent his war days in quite an indistinguishable way. He never fired his rifle in anger and the only near miss he had was when he was at Monte Cassino. He should have slept in a bombed-out church but decided it was more comfortable in his lorry. The following morning upon returning to where he should have slept, he was amazed to find a large piece of shrapnel exactly where his head would have been had he remained there. The Almighty certainly looked after him that night.

His war record proves he didn't have a particularly active time of it from 1942 to 1946 but he did end up with four medals. The War Medal 1939–1945, everybody who served had one of those. The 1935–45 Star, again many had that one too. The Italy Star because he spent some time in Sicily and Italy and the Africa Star, again as he was in Africa but his Africa Star also had a Bar or Clasp, as they call it, on the ribbon and I have been unable to find the reason for this. I am certain it wouldn't have been for gallantry, more than likely to indicate he served during a particular campaign in Africa.

He was like many ex-war veterans who did not particularly like to talk about the war. I do have a few photographs of him in uniform, just to prove he was there. On occasion he would give some snippet of detail such as for a period of the conflict he was attached to the Indian army, possibly in Italy, but I do know he has never eaten curry since the end of the war. 'Curry for breakfast, curry for lunch, curry for dinner,' he said.

In any event his war record shows that his conduct was exemplary so I assume he did, as he always would, carry out his duties in a conscientious manner, without committing to anything of spectacular note.

He became a born-again Christian probably influenced by my mother, whose family were church members at the local Mission Hall in Liverpool. My mother's aunt who my father knew already, arranged the introduction prior to my father being conscripted and from then on, he only wanted to be with her not doing his bit during the war. They kept in touch by writing, as most servicemen did at the time, and so at the end of the war and being demobbed, he again took up with Doris Pemberton and they married in 1947.

My dad had returned to his lorry-driving job with Liverpool Warehousing Company and was sent roaming, picking up a load of goods in one place and taking them to another place anywhere in the country then picking up another load to take elsewhere. My mother didn't see so much of him but it must have been long enough for my elder brother David to come along in February 1949. I followed in November 1950, a disappointment I believe as I wasn't a girl. Two children, one of each, would have been just right, for my dad in particular.

As I grew up, Dad was still roaming and when he did arrive home unannounced it was as though there was this stranger in our midst who barked orders and expected us to jump. An intrusion in our peaceful lives and into our routine became a hindrance to me especially as I got toward eight years old. Things were not comfortable when he was around. He certainly ruled the roost and even at my young age our relationship was strained. He would drag me off for a haircut, for instance, and instruct the barber to give me a short back and sides and a bit off the top. I think he thought he was still in the army! Looking at the haircuts of today, however, I do think my father inadvertently made me ahead of my time!

When I was 10 years old, we moved house. Mother was expecting again, the final try, for a daughter I believe and the final time to be disappointed.

Not long after this my grandfather started behaving oddly. My grandmother had an accident and broke her foot and was confined to hospital and during this time Grandad was doing strange things such as taking out the dog for a walk at 3.00 am. He was picked up by the police on several occasions but as there was nobody at home at this particular time, he was taken to hospital whilst enquiries were made as to the location of relatives. If memory serves me right when it was discovered that my grandmother was in hospital it was decided he should remain in another hospital. I visited him on one occasion and clearly, he wasn't himself. He swore that he was being stared at by "those two cheeky monkeys" as he put it, pointing in the direction of two tall surgical taps over a hand-wash basin opposite his bed. As a young child I didn't understand he was so unwell and just laughed but obviously as I look back there were underlying issues. The doctors eventually decided that my grandfather should be placed in an asylum. Rainhill, on the outskirts of Liverpool, was a mental hospital that was well known as the looney bin. That is where Grandad went and that is where he passed away.

I honestly believe he had then what we know now as Alzheimer's or at least some form of early-stage dementia. Goodness knows what he went through in that asylum but I was never allowed to visit him there. I reflected on Grandad's condition a lot particularly after my father's illness had been diagnosed and wondered if there was any connection, genetically. Even today there appears to be no conclusive proof one way or another if genetics are a consideration in determining the origin of this illness.

Life went on after that and my father changed his job, still as a lorry driver but he was on permanent nights, driving to London or Southampton overnight sleeping in "digs" during the day and driving back the following night. Conflict between him and me increased during my teens. His insistence that I followed his rules whilst I lived under his roof resulted in many arguments and even became physical. 'I'd never speak my father the way you speak to me' was an oft used mantra to which my reply was 'that was your problem then wasn't it?' which generally made him angrier with me.

I had been brought up to attend church each week, or should I say forced to attend church, three times on a Sunday, but as I grew older, I questioned my father's behaviour and attitude towards me as being in total contrast to what I had been taught in church. Clearly in my early teens especially I was somewhat confused. I didn't and still don't know why he was like that when I was the one son who continually gave help to him, to my mother, to anybody. Maybe he resented me as I was a son and not the daughter he longed for.

My two brothers didn't have anything like the conflict with him as I did. I was the rebel they just kowtowed to him, even to the point that growing up he insisted that my elder brother and I supported Everton Football Club, just as he done all his life but when I was old enough to make up my own mind, I supported Liverpool Football Club. This enraged him but he failed to remember that his own father supported Liverpool also and lived very close to Anfield, Liverpool's home ground.

To many this may seem of little consequence in life's bigger picture but being a red or a blue on Merseyside is a very serious business, has known to divide families and caused serious strife between friends so even at my young age when I made that momentous decision I was aware of the bad feeling it would create. In the longer term, football wasn't a subject that my father and I would talk about. It made life more peaceful.

I moved away when I was 21 buying a house some 30 miles away and didn't visit too often but the house which I bought was a little cottage in need of renovation and my father turned up with his tools willing to help and to be truthful he was good at DIY and was very helpful on many occasions. I felt the rift was starting to heal. But it would take time. Clearly, our relationship was better when we lived apart.

As time went on, we communicated regularly, met on occasion and generally played father and son but I moved to Spain for a year so we didn't talk for all that time. Eventually I called him from South Wales, it went something like this, 'Hi, Dad, I just got married!' He was dumbstruck. 'I met a lady from South Wales and I came back here with her and we got married this morning.' Silence.

Then with his mouth away from the telephone, he shouted, 'Doris, our John got married!'

Married? Married? Who to? Where is he? I couldn't help laugh, it was like an excerpt from a comedy sketch.

'I'll come up and see you and you can meet her but for now I have to go and celebrate. Bye.'

Eventually, I did visit with my wife and it was a fairly relaxed atmosphere. We returned to South Wales the same day not wishing to overstay our welcome.

Over the next few years, I kept in touch with my parents regularly. They visited us for weekends and we visited them, even being allowed to sleep in their bed. I think that was his way of showing acceptance. I made him extremely happy when I announced that my wife had given birth, to a daughter, the granddaughter he never had yet always longed for. He was, for a while, a doting grandfather particularly when the name we chose was the same as his mother, Charlotte. The first female to be born with our surname for many years.

Eventually, however, we divorced and my father's direct contact with his granddaughter was lost. I never did speak to him about how he felt but I am sure he resented me for the situation, although I know my mother kept in touch with my daughter and ex-wife for many years but as far as my father was concerned there never was another opportunity to meet her again and hold her as he wanted.

As a born-again Christian my father, and mother, disagreed with divorce and I think it took quite a while for him to accept the fact. Of course, it was all my fault in his eyes but he never did know the truth.

I remarried a few years later to my now, long suffering wife, Susan. She and my father hit it off like a house on fire so it seems my "errors" of the past had been forgotten. They even came to our wedding. Sadly, for him there was not another granddaughter or grandson for that matter.

On one of my visits to see Mum and Dad, we had a conversation about travel. I asked my dad why it was he didn't want to go on holiday abroad because since the war he hadn't ventured from these shores. 'Not really interested' was his comment, 'except the only place I would ever want to go would be the Seychelles.' I looked at him inquiringly but he never explained why, exactly, I just think I assumed because it was hot and quiet but to my detriment, I didn't follow up on it. I would possibly discover the answer at a later date but too late for him to confirm my thoughts.

My mother was listening to this conversation and she looked at me, chipping in her bit – 'Too many foreign men abroad' – and walked away.

I maintained regular contact with my folks and usually spoke to my father on a Sunday morning prior to him going to church. One particular Sunday morning, I had a conversation with him that left me baffled. Not for the first time during one of our calls in recent months, he repeated himself a couple of times, told me stories of events that he had told me before and I became concerned he was getting confused. I put down the telephone and just stood on the spot thinking about what he had just said. It wasn't anything out of the ordinary but it was just that I heard one story a few times. Susan looked at me.

'What is the matter?' she asked.

'Oh, I don't know,' I replied, 'I think my father is losing it.'

I basically brushed it off. My words were prophetic indeed. That was the day before his fall in the snow and the TIA.

During his time in hospital, his mental capacity deteriorated alarmingly. I called his consultant at Fazakerley Hospital, Liverpool and he explained to me what had happened to my dad. He said that the TIA or, more than likely TIA'S, had damaged the frontal lobe of his brain. This affected his cognitive skills, memory, language, judgement and sexual behaviours. It is in effect, the control panel of our personality. He went on to say that my father was behaving in an unacceptable way and I asked for an explanation.

The consultant told me that my father accused a doctor and a nurse of having sex on one of the beds behind the curtains. I was shocked. Furthermore, his language was appalling.

'What do you mean?' I asked.

'His foul language and suggestive comments,' he said. 'Foul language, my father using foul language? Never ever sworn in his life, never even mentioned the word s-e-x,' I said.

'It's down to the illness,' the consultant assured me, 'but it must have been in his mind or his brain in the first place.'

I knew my father had worked with many guys who were, in fact, foul mouthed and did "play around" and on more than one occasion he was asked if he had any "dirty magazines" in his lorry. I can only guess that over the years some of it did stick in his head and that Alzheimer's had been the cause of its release. Nevertheless, I could not imagine my father using that kind of language and behaving that way. It took quite some time for this massive change in him to sink in but eventually I reasoned it was probably the illness, maybe because that's what I wanted to believe.

I did actually hope that I wouldn't hear him using this bad language because, frankly, I don't know how I would have coped with that. It would, perhaps, be like coming from the mouth of another person in my dad's body. Fortunately, I never did witness him swearing and I was grateful for that.

I remember one argument I had with him years before and I happened to say, 'Well, I bloody well told you' was all I had said. He hit the roof. 'Doris, Doris, he swore at me!' Makes me smile when I think about it even now but ironic indeed.

Now here he was, allegedly, unknowingly using worse language than myself. I can't help feeling so sad that he went that way, the total opposite of how he had lived his life for the previous 79 years.

My mother wanted my father to come home from hospital, with a passion. I had to explain to her that not only would he be a danger to himself but also would be a danger to her. I had visions of him switching on the gas hob and forgetting about it and blowing up himself, my mother and the house in the process or even trying to cook something and forgetting about that and burning the place down. Additionally, my mother's life would not be her own. Who would look after him when she went out for groceries or when she went to church as clearly, he would have to be confined to the house? Mum saw the sense in what I was saying and reluctantly agreed that he should remain where he was.

He spent several months in the hospital having tests and observation whilst the authorities sought a place in a care home. After a prolonged thorough search around Merseyside two options emerged. The first was a place that housed people who had mental and emotional issues and some had also been violent offenders. This, for me, was not even an option. The thought that my dad would be grouped with people like that was quite scary. He would never survive in that environment as in one way he was quite naïve of that side of life but in another way, there were always people everywhere who would be ready to jump at the chance to take advantage of a vulnerable individual in situations like this and my dad certainly was vulnerable. The second option seemed to be a decent enough care home. My mother went to visit and was informed that there were activities for residents including a garden to tend plants and flowers, which had been a passion of my dad for many years. All the plus points were highlighted and my mother called me to tell me she had selected this particular residential care home.

Arrangements were made and Susan and myself gathered together different things for him, such as duvet covers with matching pillow cases, with the great help of Susan's mum, Marie, who gave him a selection of various sweaters also. We went to the home taking all we had brought, each item having had his name sewn into them and we put them in his room. He was well equipped for his new home.

Susan and I went to visit Dad one Saturday not that long after he had moved in and even then, there was a noticeable change in his personality. He seemed remote but we tried to engage with him, chatting as normally as we could. He was largely unresponsive so I took him to the television area where there was nobody else around and, knowing there was a heavyweight boxing match on, which he used to be very interested in, sat him down in front of the TV. I was chatting enthusiastically to him about the fight as we watched but when I turned to him, he was fast asleep. I felt deflated and frustrated so I went to one of the care staff who assured me that she would take care of him when he woke up. Susan and I left in silence, with something of a cloud of depression hanging over us. Then again, what did I really expect?

Pretty soon after that, things started to go wrong.

It was clear, more or less from the outset, that there were no activities for residents no garden to speak of and no flowers to attend to and the organisation of laundry was appalling. Within a few weeks the matching duvet covers and pillowslips had disappeared along with several other things including most of the sweaters. We complained without success but alarmingly, my father one day was wearing somebody else's clothes, even shoes that were the wrong size, so wrong that he could hardly walk. Some clothes in his wardrobe were damp as were other items left on a rack in the corridor. It became obvious this was such a badly run care home.

Other items disappeared including his watch and spectacles. He was at this point somewhat oblivious to all this. Then to our horror we arrived at the care home, on 8 February 2003 to see my father's face covered in bruises. I enquired as to what had happened to him and was told that he fell over a rolled-up carpet and landed on his face but these injuries were totally inconsistent with that, far worse, in fact. My mother informed me that my father had told her the "boys" came into his room last night and beat him up.

When he referred to the "boys" he was always referring to myself and my elder brother. In his confused mind he clearly had imagined his "boys" had beaten him up but the truth, in my opinion, is much darker than that. Had he suffered abuse? Clearly, it's not unheard of in care homes. I tried to see the person who was in charge of the home but was told she was not available. We also noticed a number of bruises on the back of his hands. If I needed any confirmation that my father had been abused, I believe this was it as I was convinced that these bruises were compatible with being hit on the back of the hand but I still had no tangible proof.

The reason I know it was on 8 February 2003 was because this was his 80th birthday and along with a few relatives we celebrated with tea and cake and my father seemed to come alive. His speech was somewhat more coherent, he had his two favourite ladies in the world with him, my mother and her aunt who had introduced them and he showed his affection to them both.

Sadly, this was done with my father looking as though he had just stepped out of a boxing ring after being in there with Joe Frazier.

Susan said to him, 'How about a piece of your chocolate birthday cake?'

He looked at her before replying, 'What are you trying to do, make me fat?' A comment that made us all smile but in a sad way not that he knew. He was never to be so happy again.

There appeared to be relatives of other residents who had similar stories to tell, of the treatment that their loved one's had been receiving. My mother spoke to one lady whose husband was not unlike my father and pretty quickly word spread. A meeting was demanded with the lady who ran the home and I wanted to attend but my elder brother said he would take care of it. It was a major mistake by me not to go. Nothing was resolved, everything was denied and in my opinion my mother and brother had not been forceful enough in finding answers, which was a similar story from relatives of other residents. Those poor people in care had been let down, not just by the staff who were supposed to provide care in a safe environment but by the relatives who were supposed to be standing up for them as their representatives, their voices, their guardians at a time when it mattered most but those relatives failed. Failed to ask questions, failed to find answers, failed to protect their loved ones and, I have no option but to include myself as one of those who failed. I can only offer my very belated apologies, if it were possible. If my words come across here as being angry, I make no excuse for that.

Although it was obvious there was a lack of care in this home, it is, so I have found out since, not confined to this particular establishment. Not every care home is run like this, of course, but speaking to friends and relatives over the years made me realise that the word care is missing in a number of homes. Whether this is due to unsuitable and unqualified staff being paid the minimum wage or just the owners wanting to profit with the high fees and low expenditure is debatable. Maybe it is a mixture of both. Certainly, it is clear that the percentage of "professional carers" is low in comparison to wage earners just doing a job. Conscientious carers are limited but are vital to the overall welfare of residents. Indeed, my mother spent her last months in care with vascular dementia being just one of her conditions, but was so well looked after and nursed and cared for by some of those conscientious people who are priceless in today's society.

My dad's condition deteriorated over the following months and it was obvious there was going to be only one outcome not too far in the distance. I visited as often as I could but sitting next to the bed of someone totally unresponsive and continually sleeping is not the easiest thing to do, as I am sure many people can attest to. Each visit became a sadder event powerless to do anything to help. It was just a case of waiting. It is true what people say when they refer to end of life care being worse for humans than animals. We take the brave decision to euthanize our loving precious animal companions but are unable to ease the suffering of real people. I do understand the call for assisted dying here in UK. When there is no hope of recovery, no chance of providing a life with quality, what is the alternative? Each individual will have their own opinions and thoughts, I have no doubt.

In the meantime, we understood that the lady who ran the home had, all of a sudden, taken a position in Australia and one of the caring staff, who was my chief suspect in the attack on my father, had left his job. Now it was obvious we were never going to get answers. At that point did we want any answers? I'm not so sure. I do know however, that my father's possessions were depleted and nobody had owned up to it, nobody took responsibility. An extremely sad situation at the closure of any life.

On 27 December 2003 my telephone at home rang. It was my younger brother. 'My dad's dead' was his opening line. Not a shock but delivered without any compassion whatsoever. He and my mother were with him when he passed away, if that is of any comfort, not that he was aware of his surroundings. The last time I saw him he was thin, wrinkled and his breathing was shallow and laboured, it made me remember him when he was working, when I was young at a time, when there was no containerised transport of goods. It was all sheets and ropes and my father had muscles, real hard muscles and heavy calloused hands having refused to wear gloves when roping in all weathers. Now here he was at deaths door not even half the man he used to be.

I like to think he was hovering at heaven's gate re-assuring my mother that everything he had lived his life for was about to be realised and he soon would be meeting his God to whom he had devoted so much of his life, and furthermore, he would be reunited with my mother in the fullness of time just as they both always believed it would be.

Alzheimer's disease is such a cruel illness. In some cases, such as my father it can be worse than having cancer. My late father-in-law, Ivor, had been diagnosed with lung cancer and was ill for five months until he succumbed to that dreadful illness. My dad lingered for nearly two years deteriorating most of the time and the affect wasn't just on him but those that were watching him go downhill unable to do anything to halt the downward spiral, my mother and brothers, myself, aunts and uncles, friends, especially from the church, and nursing staff at the care home.

The journey from South Wales to Liverpool for his funeral was not without incident. The weather was atrocious, very heavy rain and strong winds. We headed over the Severn Bridge between Wales and England with Susan's mother accompanying us. The bridge is well known for being adversely affected when it is windy, you can actually feel it sway, and I am not sure why it hadn't been closed but we carried on without a word being said. I think Susan and her mother held their collective breath all the time we were on the bridge. For them it certainly was a white-knuckle ride. Under different circumstances I'd probably have driven slower just to elongate the tension.

'If it wasn't my dad's funeral,' I said, 'I'd turn around and go home!'

We arrived in Liverpool unscathed but relieved as the weather had eased on the way up north.

The funeral took place in January 2004 and it said a lot for my dad that the church was packed. It was officiated by my mother's younger brother William, or to give him his correct title, Pastor William Joseph Pemberton of Bethany Baptist Chapel, Fazakerley, Liverpool. Ironically, Uncle Bill, as I knew him, also passed away as a result of Alzheimer's disease in 2009. This disease does not discriminate against just who it affects.

The opening hymn of the service was one my dad had asked me to include in his Last Will and Testament when I prepared it years before. "Lead Kindly Light" was a favourite of his with the final two lines "to rest forever after earthly strife, in the calm light of everlasting life". *Very appropriate*, I thought.

Uncle Bill's sermon was impressive, as they always were. He was preaching and referring to somebody he had known for much of his life, being a lot younger than my mother. Uncle Bill was well known for his powerful, meaningful sermons and I know, in better times, my father would have been absorbed by the words he used. My dad was great admirer of Uncle Bill and his preaching. It was in part a eulogy and a sermon and towards the end of the service the sun broke through the clouds shining through the window directly onto my dad's coffin. Coincidence? Or the belief that it was at that point when my father's spirit truly entered into the kingdom of God? We all have our thoughts, opinions and beliefs, take from that what you will.

Dad, Mum, Auntie May

Cared for in a care home

Chapter 2
The Poster

There is no failure except in no longer trying.
– Elbert Hubbard

Life went on much as it usually does, even after bereavement. Mother decided she needed to move house as the garden was too big where she had lived with Dad so she relocated to a warden-controlled apartment. Ideal for her to be able to mix with others, she was able to drive and continued to attended her church regularly, which was vital to her wellbeing.

I would visit when I could but before doing so would always stop off at Allerton Cemetery to visit my dad's grave and maybe clean it up, Susan would put flowers on and I would cut the grass around the headstone. I can't say every visit was sad as I took consolation that although his shell lay in the ground below me, his soul was at peace wrapped in the love of his God who he deeply believed in and will stay there for all eternity. I hope for him he was right.

One day in 2007, Susan came home from work. She handed me a folded piece of paper. Opening it I was confronted with the title "KILIMANJARO TREK", "Climb the highest freestanding mountain in the world, raising money for The Alzheimer's Society".

I studied it for a minute and looked up. 'You are joking, aren't you?' I said.

'Well, it came in the mail at work and I just wondered' was the reply.

I folded up the poster and put it on my desk and nothing more was said.

Historically I had been very sporty through my school days, late teens, into my 20s usually playing football twice a week but basically giving up in my early 30s and taking up smoking instead. Sport almost became a thing of the past except for one or two occasions when I was asked to turn out for this team or that. Largely life consisted of working, smoking, drinking and, always, laughter.

In 2005, under the influence of a few glasses of wine I borrowed a skateboard. Where we live is situated on a steep hill. "Skateboard and hill go well" was my irrational thought. Marching up the driveway, skateboard tucked under my arm I was at the top of the hill. Putting it down on the floor I wondered what part of me was going to get hurt, cut, broken or all three.

Susan, along with our neighbour and her son were watching from the garden above me. I heard the neighbour say to her son, 'John shouldn't be doing this, he is not wearing a helmet or knee pads or elbow pads. I don't want to see you doing this, you understand?'

'Yes, Mother' came the reply.

Down the hill I went. It was going rather fast I remember but it didn't last too long. Then wipe out! The skateboard went one way I went the other. The skateboard continued down the hill but I came to an abrupt stop in the middle of the lane lying on my back, laughing. Just then a large 4 x 4 come over the crest of the hill and I moved quickly to get out of the way. I say quickly, I mean quickly in a painful way. The bottom of my back had been the first thing to make contact with the tarmac and I swear I bounced. There was no grazing just a sharp pain near the base of my spine. Still, I think the alcohol had kept the worst of the pain at bay because the following morning I was extremely sore in my lower back area. All my own fault I know so didn't expect any sympathy and didn't get any either.

I didn't go rushing off to see the doctor but waited a while to see if it settled down on its own. Clearly though, there was a problem and in due course I visited the doctor who referred me to a specialist where scans along with X-rays were carried out. The diagnosis was that I had a displaced, or slipped, disc in my lower back and a discectomy or lumbar decompression surgery was required to put it right. This is the procedure where the removal of all or a portion of the intervertebral disc that is pressing on a nerve in the spinal cord is required, to relieve the pain and give back feeling down my right leg and in my foot that I'd lost.

In 2006, this was carried out with no problems arising. Susan and her mother visited me on the night of the surgery and whilst I remember their visit I was under the influence of morphine, it's actually better than alcohol, for the pain. This resulted in me trying to entice Susan into bed with me, in front of her mother and loud enough for the rest of the ward and their visitors to hear. How embarrassing! I don't remember much after that although the following morning one or two of the other patients grinned in my direction and it took me a while to remember that the evening before I'd behaved like a right pratt.

The nursing staff and physiotherapists had me up and slowly walking but generally I was feeling quite good. I had to walk up and down a flight of stairs to be able to be discharged from hospital that day. This was duly carried out without much effort and I called Susan to pick me up which she did. Great to get out of the hospital and home again.

Once home, Susan looked at the scar on my back which was covered by a vertical piece of sticky plaster that hid the now-glued incision. To her surprise the skin around the scar was red, black and blue in a very wide area. She photographed it so I could see what it looked like.

'Hey,' I said, 'maybe one of the theatre staff beat me up when I was under anaesthetic.'

'Don't be ridiculous,' she snapped. 'This was a big operation so you were bound to be pulled about.'

The discolouration became worse over the next few days but I took things easy, exercised as instructed by the physiotherapist and generally acted sensible, which was completely out of character for me. I was unable to drive for a minimum of two weeks so had to get used to my own company, except when I was chauffeured to the hospital for a weekly "waste of time" physio appointment. I say waste of time because all the appointment consisted of was a couple of questions and then the physiotherapist gave me a couple of freehand drawings of exercises I should be doing. I don't have a degree in the blinking obvious but it was clear what I needed to do. Strengthen the core, gradually use my back more doing gentle sit-ups, bending, balance over a large inflated medical ball, just doing things easy and building myself up.

However, during this time I fell into what I believe was a short-term depression. Susan would leave for work in the morning and I would be in my bathrobe usually sitting at the table but when she returned, I was in exactly the same position not having even bothered to shower or change. This went on for several days and I cannot explain why. I was able to prepare food in the evening but that was the extent of my exercise. After a few days of this I decided to give myself a thorough emotional examination followed by a stern talking to. I felt better already so took a deep breath, had a shower and changed and looked presentable when Susan arrived home that evening.

After two weeks I was back driving. Doing normal things helped, such as going to work or meeting friends for a drink and generally socialising again.

That's when I got to thinking. Why do I want to smoke? It is a disgusting habit, made me smell like an ashtray and at that time smokers were becoming pariahs of society, with a ban on smoking in pubs and restaurants only 12 months away. So there and then I made the decision to quit.

With a little help from my GP, I went to a couple of meetings at the local community hospital, designed to give advice, guidance and discussion as well as handing out nicotine patches if required. I found these meetings to be very helpful but I was quite surprised when I walked into the room the first time. There were about a dozen people but I was the only male! Maybe men don't want to give it up, or can't but some ladies need to because they are pregnant perhaps or many other reasons. Anyway, the first thing I was instructed to do was to blow into a tube with a gauge on it. This was an Exhaled Carbon Monoxide Test. The gauge went up to 100 and I blew into it. The reading was about 95. The lady undertaking the test said, 'You've just had a cigarette, haven't you?'

I confessed I had just put one out before I came in. Carbon Monoxide is a poisonous gas that you cannot see, smell or taste but it is present in cigarettes, as well as other things like exhaust fumes and faulty gas boilers. Why on earth did I want to inhale that? It turned out to be the final cigarette I have ever had to this day.

On my second visit I blew into the tube and it read 5 on the gauge.

'Why?' I asked.

'It's OK,' she replied, 'that will be the level in the air or maybe you walked past a car with the engine running Carbon Monoxide in the fumes.'

I felt relieved and proud that I had taken this first positive step.

I was given a lot of information from NHS sources about how your body recovers from smoking and at what stages you feel the benefit and found it encouraging. For instance, after 20 minutes your pulse should slow and not race as it does when you have a cigarette. After eight hours oxygen levels will have increased in your body and 48 hours later Carbon Monoxide has gone. After 72 hours breathing is eased and after two weeks your blood will be pumping better. Then, after three months breathing has improved and lung function will have increased. After 10 years, you have halved the chance of having a heart attack in comparison to a smoker. I followed each of these changes in my body and can say that I did feel better without a cigarette both physically and psychologically. I wore patches on my arm for about a week but felt confident enough I could stop smoking without using them.

I can honestly say it was no effort at all to give up the dreaded weed and with the exercises I had to continue to do to strengthen my back and not now poisoning myself with Carbon Monoxide I really was starting to feel better about myself too. I found out that for most people the temptation to have a cigarette is fleeting, it really only lasts for seconds. If temptation stepped in my path, I learned to divert away from it by thinking of something different or doing something that guided me away from the thought. It was a revelation to me that when it mattered, I did have strong will power and a determination to succeed. Perhaps I should have examined myself and lifestyle like that a long time before. I now firmly believe that good did come out of self-created adversity and possible destruction.

So, in 2007 after the poster had been laid before me, at home alone, I gave serious, careful consideration to taking up the challenge of climbing Mount Kilimanjaro. Even though smoking was history and my back was much better I was far from being fit enough to complete this monumental task. I needed to think about it longer.

Susan and I never spoke about it, I had assumed she had completely forgotten about the poster but it was at the forefront of my mind almost continually, even waking in the middle of the night, staring into the darkness of our bedroom and trying to imagine what it would be like. Was I up for it?

In time I had my answer. I had made my decision on my own, it was too good an opportunity to let pass by. After all, when did I ever back away from a challenge, even one that was off the planet in comparison to other challenges I have faced? Can't remember even one.

Susan arrived home from work. I looked at her and she could see I had something rather momentous to say, I could see it in her eyes.

'Paid my deposit,' I blurted out.

'You've done what?' she replied rather shocked.

'Paid my deposit, I'm going to climb Kili!'

'Oh, what have you done?' was her immediate reply. I told her that I telephoned the Alzheimer's Society and it was explained to me that I pay £250 deposit now to reserve my place then I have the option of paying for the trip myself and all donations I collect go directly to the society or I deduct the cost of the trip from donations and the balance goes to Alzheimer's. I opted to pay for the trip myself. I found the alternative option to be incompatible with my way of thinking about how funds are raised for charity. Susan was in full agreement with this but I'm sure at that point she must have questioned the wisdom in bringing home that poster in the first place.

'So, what is your next step?' she enquired.

'Well, I need some plans, a fitness plan and a fund-raising plan, and I don't think it's going to be easy,' I admitted. 'I have 13 months to get fit and get sponsored.'

Within a few days I'd received the documentation from Alzheimer's Society giving all the necessary details of dates, times, a map of the route up Kilimanjaro and down, kit suggestions and recommendations, along with the very important sponsorship forms. I studied the map intently and went through the itinerary in detail.

We would be leaving UK to fly overnight to Nairobi, Kenya on 19 September 2008 from there we would take the 50 minutes flight to Kilimanjaro Airport. We were scheduled to return on 27 September 2008 overnight arriving back in London the following morning.

The information supplied by the organisers was very informative. Not that I had any reason to know before now but I hadn't realised, for instance, that there are several routes up and down Kilimanjaro and we would be taking The Machame Route, (otherwise known as "the whiskey route", hard and rough maybe, purely as it is regarded as tougher than another route, The Marangu Route which is known as the Coca Cola route, soft and fizzy I guess), and to ascend and descend via The Mweka Route. It would take us six days up and down all being well and we were to sleep in two man tents each night. All catering would be done for us and porters would transport our belongings except what we would carry ourselves in our day sacks or rucksacks.

I must confess, even though this was my first trek of this kind I was impressed by how organised things appeared to be. There would also be a training weekend organised in North Wales during May 2008. We were now in August 2007 I needed some serious exercising very quickly if I was even going to make that weekend. North Wales' mountains are unforgiving to the untrained and ill prepared so things needed to happen fast.

Chapter 3
Training and Fundraising

By failing to prepare you are preparing to fail.
– Benjamin Franklin

What would I do to raise sponsorship? A quick brainstorm with Susan was a start.

We listed a number of possible things that we could organise to raise enough money to make it worth the effort needed.

A cricket match in the village? Historically, as a village we have regularly hosted an annual fund-raiser in a local farmers' field with drinks, burgers, hot dogs and cakes for sale, for the benefit of one charity or the other. I was sure I could gather interest in that. Tickets could be sold via the local pub/restaurant, The Woodlands Tavern, courtesy of owners Keith and Sue, and selling house to house as we had done in previous years. After the cricket maybe we could organise an auction at The Woodlands asking people to donate items to be put into the sale? General requests from family and friends for donations? Also, I would approach clients of my business. I am sure they would be happy to help. Susan could also ask her work colleagues. Really, if I was going to do this over the next 12 months it had to be financially very beneficial to

Alzheimer's Society. It was clearly going to be hard work raising funds, working, training and generally living life. I hoped that it was going to be the best time ever, if I was successful in pulling it all off. In fact, the next 12 months would be like no other year in my life.

Another event in the village takes place each November. Bonfire night and fireworks display has always been very popular, during which time we barbeque and sell burgers and the like whilst my job is usually becoming the pyro-technician for the night. One of the organisers, Liz, suggested the profits of November 2007 bonfire and fireworks display should go to my fundraising for Alzheimer's disease. A wonderful gesture and it would be the first event towards my goal. I didn't have any fundraising target in mind when I set out to take on this challenge but it had to be in the thousands.

One of the local farmers, Alun, suggested we have the bonfire in one of his fields located in the centre of the village. I was grateful for that as in previous years it had been on the outskirts of the village making it more work and logistically more difficult to transport all the items needed. On top of that Alun was involved with the Young Farmers group and took a number of tickets to sell to those people. I really didn't know how many people would turn up but was sure the Young Farmers would boost the numbers as well as the takings for beer and burgers.

Another local farmer, Stuart, who I got on particularly well with, helped sort out the bonfire, set the safety fencing in place and generally ran around in his tractor making sure everything was as it should be to comply with health and safety regulations. In previous years, Stuart and I would go off onto the local estate in his tractor to find firewood, with the blessing of the estate's owners, of course. I was like a child in a sweet shop riding around in the tractor. Hang on, how old am I? It was great fun, the highlight of bonfire night but sadly we were to lose Stuart unexpectedly a few years later. Bonfire night could never be the same again, for me. He was a remarkable man, Stuart, always ready to help, give advice or just listen. Something special dropped out of my life and the lives of others when Stuart passed away.

5 November 2007 arrived and everything was in place. I was amazed to see just how many people attended swelled by the Young Farmers who were, let me say, "enthusiastic" particularly when the fireworks went off and the beer was on sale. The barbeque did well, Stuart ensured that the bonfire was ablaze with Guy Fawkes sitting on the top and it turned out to be a really good fun night for adults and children, as well as being very well supported and a complete success. I had started on my fundraising journey. We adjourned to the Woodlands, muddy boots lined up outside and us stinking of wood smoke, for a well-earned beer or several. Now what about the small matter of getting myself fit?

I have a friend, Andrew, who is ex-army and very fit. Experienced in survival in the wild, he offered to set me on the road to fitness. It had to be a gradual process, building up my stamina, fitness and mental strength. He knew all too well what level I had to be to achieve this unlikely goal.

We started off by walking locally into Wentwood Forest and Gray Hill which were a mixture of distance walks and hill climbs. I then progressed my development by going alone. One Saturday in the November, Susan decided to come with me. We walked a while just "following our noses" but realised after a few hours that we didn't actually know where we were.

It was late afternoon and the darkness was setting in and I was starting to get a little concerned, being surrounded only by fields, trees and hills. As luck would have it, we saw in the distance a house, an old farmhouse as it turned out, so I had no alternative but to knock on the door. It was answered eventually by an elderly chap who clearly was a farmer, judging by his clothes, his manner and the flock of geese milling around the farmyard.

I apologised for disturbing him and went on to explain where I needed to get to. He roared with laughter!

'Just head down that path, keep going and don't divert off it,' he said after he'd calmed down, 'over a few stiles and you'll be there in 20 minutes.'

I thanked him and off we set in the direction he had gestured. We clearly had become disorientated as to the direction we had headed in but it seems we managed to go around in almost a complete circle. As he said, 20 minutes later we were back home, I was so grateful for that man's help. The lesson I learned from that was, always take a mobile telephone with me and I could, at least make contact with Andrew, signal permitting, as he knew the area so well.

Andrew decided that I was making progress so suggested we climbed Pen-y-Fan, the highest point in the Brecon Beacons National Park. The beacons are approximately 900 square kilometres and include the Black Mountain to the west and Ffores Fawr and consist of stunning landscapes and views. However, Brecon is also known as the training ground for military personnel, especially for those who want to become involved in the Special Forces. It is not so much that Pen-y-Fan is high or, indeed steep, it is actually an easy climb but the soldiers going through special assessment usually carry massive backpacks along with, at times, parts of heavy ordnance as well as their own weapons. It certainly is not for the faint hearted.

Pen-y-Fan stands at 886 metres and is the highest British Peak south of Snowdonia in North Wales. It has an adjacent mountain called Corn Du at 873 metres so we decided to head for the summit of Pen-y-Fan then on our way down we would visit the summit of Corn Du.

I thought I handled the first climb quite well and discovered at the summit of Pen-y-Fan there are magnificent 360-degree views when clear as it was that day, and looking down was able to see the town of Brecon and surrounding area.

However, Pen-y-Fan is dangerous. High winds, unpredictable weather and heavy mist and fog can be hazardous even for experienced climbers and indeed, lives have been lost on Pen-y-Fan including mountain rescue personnel.

On occasions on subsequent visits when Andrew and I, and others, climbed Pen-y-Fan I have known him to stop people attempting to ascend and point out that they are ill-equipped to climb, as many think it is an easy stroll. His argument is sound.

'Why should any mountain rescue people put their lives at risk just because you are unprepared for the conditions?' Usually, the individuals would about turn and walk back to the bottom.

At the end of my first climb and at the bottom of the mountain drinking a cup of tea, it suddenly dawned on me that just a short time before I would never have dreamed that I would be climbing like this. Never in my wildest imagination could I have considered doing this but here I was I'd been to the top of Pen-y-Fan and Corn Du, not the hardest or the most technically difficult of climbs but I had conquered them. An achievement, the first of many I hoped.

Training

I was in need of a new pair of walking boots as I could see that the training was getting serious and I obviously needed the right equipment. Andrew and I headed into Brecon town centre where there are numerous shops selling the whole range of outdoor gear. From climbing ropes to canoes, boots to wet weather gear, head torches to Kendal Mint Cake. We went into one shop and I chose a pair which, when I put them on felt perfect, very comfortable, and a really good and popular make that didn't need any "running-in" time. I settled on these but just as I was about to pay for them Andrew chipped in.

'No, John, I'm buying these for you as my contribution to your event.'

I was totally shocked. What a wonderful gesture and thanked him so much. Not only was he helping me train and get fit in his own time but also financially contributing to support me and my effort. It is hard, even now, for me to put into words just how that made me feel. I suppose in one way it added to the pressure to successfully complete the climb but also there and then increased my commitment to the project.

During this time, I discovered there had been a documentary shown on BBC Wales about a group of Welsh ex-rugby players who took on the challenge of climbing Kilimanjaro. I was frustrated at not having seen it as I thought it might be pertinent to me and helpful and, of course, catch-up TV wasn't around in those days. So, I called BBC Wales in Cardiff and explained the situation. They were very helpful supplying me with the name and address of the production company. I contacted them and told them what I was up to and without delay they very happily sent me a DVD of the programme. I was so grateful for their assistance. It was enlightening to say the least and helped me see at first hand just what struggles lay ahead. Clearly, it was going to be tough and this was highlighted by the fact that not all of them made it to the summit. These tough, hard ex-rugby guys didn't all complete the challenge. For a moment, a small hint of doubt flittered through my mind but it was only for a solitary moment. They are they and I am me. Different, don't compare.

Over the weeks and months, the tempo of my training increased a lot. I was going out often on my own and decided I needed to do some walking and climbing in the dark. One particular morning, I went out at 2.00 am and headed up to Gray Hill and then on to the forest. Between the trees, heading up the hill it was, naturally, pitch black and I only had my head torch to show me the way ahead, along a path I had by now trodden many times. I was aware that there was something to my left about ten metres away, and whatever it was, moved silently. I cannot explain how I knew there was something there but I just had a feeling that I wasn't alone.

I stopped, turned my head and the light picked out two bright yellow eyes staring back at me. I wasn't startled or afraid but I was curious. I turned back toward the path and continued walking.

After about 100, or so, metres I stopped again and turned my head to my left. I looked and it looked with blinking eyes, the same two yellow eyes. It had been walking parallel to me at my pace. I liked this so I continued walking. Once again, I stopped further along the path, and looked. Still there! Still staring! Still following! It was an exciting experience. It could only have been a deer so no alarm and I didn't even give a thought that I was in any danger of maybe being attacked, more than that it was comforting to have a travel companion even for a short while, then without a sound it scuttled off into the darkness never to be seen again. Was it my dad or maybe a relative or friend just keeping their eyes on me? Depends on what you believe I suppose but it was an enthralling experience.

The company organising the challenge informed me that there was to be a training weekend in North Wales; a chance to walk and climb in Snowdonia National Park and to meet my fellow trekkers. So, in April 2008 I headed up to Capel Curig, one early Friday morning excited about putting my newfound fitness and stamina to the test. We were to stay for two nights in a Youth Hostel which, when I arrived, I found was exactly for youths and not for a 57-year-old trying to recapture something from the past, if that's what I was doing. It was quite basic with a number of bunk beds in each room. Obviously, there were separate rooms for males and females. I wasn't quick enough and ended up with one of the top bunks while the younger elements grabbed the lower bunks. That's consideration for you!

We made our acquaintances and headed out for our first trek around Snowdonia.

This is where I made my first mistake. I had bought a very expensive down-filled jacket obviously to keep warm on Kilimanjaro but in North Wales on a wet cold misty morning it was totally useless. One of the organisers pointed out that the wet weather forecast would ruin it so I had little option but to roll it up and stashed it in my backpack. Fortunately, along the way was an outdoor activity shop and I was able to purchase a warm and storm-proof jacket. Just as well. A little later, Jupiter the weather god, wreaked havoc on us and made it hammer down.

The treks we undertook that weekend were tougher than I had been doing so far but I learned a lot in the different terrain than I had been used to. I was happy that I had been able to keep up with the group even though at times I was a little short of breath. Somebody remarked about my heavy breathing and all I could do is gasp, 'Ex-smoker!' I felt overall I had equipped myself well and this then gave me confidence. My optimism rose after that weekend. I was going to succeed.

Back home I continued my daily routines of training, walking and, of course, working. I hadn't been so active for years and was really enjoying it.

I would go out on different routes frequently getting lost but eventually finding my way back to where I should be or by finding a person whose knowledge of the area was far greater than mine, although the places where I was walking was definitely devoid of people, so on at least two occasions I was lucky to have found somebody miles from nowhere at stupid o'clock in the morning. On one occasion in the forest, I turned down a path and after a couple of minutes I knew I had taken a wrong turning. I turned around and spotted in the grass a £5 note. Call it fate if you wish but that £5 went into my sponsorship fund so maybe there was a reason that I was guided to take that wrong path.

Fundraising was also at the centre of my efforts. I had done quite a bit of fundraising and organising events to raise money for various charities over the years so I was no stranger to it. Previous efforts had included things like organising '60s' nights where people dressed up in 1960s clothes and I hired a band that played '60s' music. Very successful. I also undertook a fixed line solo parachute jump, for the first time, as well as modelling with professional models on a catwalk. When I was asked to do this, I just assumed they were short of real models but it was fun, raised a lot of money and I'd done something I had never ever imagined I'd ever do. In hindsight, I really must have looked like a right pratt. However, as anybody involved in fundraising will attest, it is hard work. I addressed members of the family first sending a sponsorship form to my mother and asking her to raise as much as she could from family in Liverpool and surrounding areas and of course church members. My uncle, the very well respected church-minister, had been diagnosed with Alzheimer's at this time so the subject was close to the hearts of his congregation.

One evening, I was alone at home whilst Susan visited her mother overnight. I did what I normally do when alone and had a glass of wine. This was quickly followed by several others. An idea came into my head, I know not why, I know not how, but in the quiet solitude of home, thinking about the climb, words started to form in my mind in the shape of a song. It is probably the kind of idea that could only come into my head when under the influence of the grape. I grabbed a pencil and paper and, standing in the kitchen wrote things that came into my mind. It really didn't take too long before I had the lyrics written, as they seemed to flow quite easily and so I went to my study and sat down with my guitar. Now, I am no super star guitarist by any stretch of the imagination although I have been known to sing in the odd public performance, so I strummed around a bit but by then I was getting alcohol induced tired so decided to leave it for the time being.

When I awoke the following morning, I remembered the events of previous evening but basically dismissed the idea of writing a song. Until, that is, I sat down a little later in the morning and read what I had written. The words were meaningful, emotional and I knew then I couldn't forget it, even if it was just to satisfy my own curiosity. Picking up my guitar again, I started with a simple 3-chord tune and practised a few times. Then put it down to do some work returning to it again later in the day.

Fundraising cricket match

When Susan returned home and I presented it to her. I sang it she read the words and she thought it was OK. It was never going to be number one in the charts but hey if it raises some money then all well and good. "Every Step of the Way" was born. It turned out, rather by accident than design, that the song actually doesn't have to apply to me climbing a mountain. The words can appeal to life in general or whatever the listener might like to imagine given a particular situation or traumatic event, for instance, so I have been told. I practised a lot and just about got it all in my head but what was I going to do with it now? The answer was around the corner.

I started to organise a cricket match with the agreement of a local farmer, Andy, who owns the flattest field around. I had organised matches before and it was more of a comic event, than a serious match. We had sold beer, soft drinks, barbecued burgers and sausages as well as having games, raffle and one or two other fund-raising initiatives with all profits going to the particular cause I was raising funds for that year. There was no reason why I couldn't do it again.

Firstly, I needed players, not too serious and looking for some fun on a Saturday afternoon. On top of that I decided to arrange an auction in the evening at the Woodlands Tavern and asked people for donations to the Auction.

In the meantime, I designed and printed tickets for the cricket match and went about selling them door to door and over the bar at the Woodlands. Tickets sales went well even some people buying tickets but saying they couldn't attend. Such generosity. Donations in the form of auction lots arrived also. I was overwhelmed by the kindness from many people. We had auction lots such as a four-ball game of golf with a professional golfer, paintings, variety of wines, a family photograph portrait by my friend Andrew, who is a professional photographer in his other life, and he also donated a voucher for a helicopter ride for two and a voucher for a drive in an Aston Martin. I would add to this that Andrew was immense in his support for me providing "Every Step of the Way" caps, pens and T Shirts. There was other donated lots such as Waterford Crystal, mountain bikes, a family meal at Woodlands Tavern, courtesy of Keith and Sue and rugby posters to mention but a few, included in a total of 30 lots. I could not thank people enough.

It occurred to me that this was an ideal opportunity to sing "Every Step of the Way" prior to the auction to open up proceedings and unleash my musical talent on an unsuspecting world! Well, to be honest, to emphasise why I was doing this just in case anybody didn't realise the important personal connection I had to this project.

So, on Saturday 2 August 2008 the cricket match took place. I was panicking a little in the morning as the weather didn't look too good at all and whilst ticket sales had been encouraging, I really wanted people to attend and have fun. As if by magic the clouds cleared, the sun shone and everybody turned up. My mother and my aunt came down from Liverpool spending a while on the gate to inspect tickets or sell them to anybody who was without one. I'd had a number of t-shirts made entitled "John's Every Step of the Way Trek" and both Mum and my aunt were wearing one each, as were a number of friends as well as myself and Susan. I must say they looked quite good with the map of Africa on the front pinpointing the location of Kilimanjaro and "Leading the Fight against Dementia, The Alzheimer's Society" on the back. I also had made some wristbands with, of course, "Every Step of the Way" Kilimanjaro 2008 engraved on them. One size each for males and females. The sad part about that was I could only buy them in small numbers from Australia, believe it or not. It seemed, at the time the minimum number I had to buy in UK was 500 and I was never going to give them away let alone sell that many, but on top of that, to add insult to injury, I had to pay import tax on the Australian wristbands too!

Both Mum and Aunt immersed themselves in the whole event. It was a fun filled afternoon with the help of some of the villagers serving the drinks and food, cooked over the barbeque by Susan's friend Aileen, as well as selling raffle tickets, again with prizes generously donated by many. I have no idea who won the cricket match but it did not matter. Later on, we cleared away and retired to the Woodlands for a buffet before the auction.

I asked a friend, Steve, (who sadly passed away recently as I write) to be auctioneer having been impressed by his performance at another charity auction a few years before. Prior to the start of the auction, I informed those gathered that I would be singing a song I had written in memory of my father and to highlight my up-and-coming task of climbing Mount Kilimanjaro. So, I picked up my guitar and got it under way.

As I sang, I was looking around and could see the emotion of the song affected some, with several tears being shed. It was, generally, well received. My aunt remarked later that it could be a hymn whilst others advised me to record it. I was pleased with the reaction.

I had made a display board with photographs of people who had been affected by or passed away with Alzheimer's disease which was there for all to see. Apart from my father there were pictures of my grandfather, my uncle, who was living with it at that time, friend's parents and relatives, some of whom I'd never met. These photographs, I had decided, will be with me when I summit Kilimanjaro, so whilst I was doing it in memory of my dad, it was also to remember others who also had cruelly been struck down by Alzheimer's and carrying their memories from the past with a lot of hope for the future.

The auction got under way with much interest from those attending. The outcome was that every lot was sold and raised a total of £2,065 which was far beyond my wildest dreams. I can only, even now, thank those who contributed in any way whatsoever.

In the meantime, my training continued with me stepping up the distances I walked and visiting Pen-y-Fan more often. Pushing myself hard in all weathers and times of day often alone but totally focused on my goal. Riding my exercise bicycle in my garage playing music in my headphones, switched off from the world and immersed totally in what I was doing. It was the only way to succeed.

I thought about the advice I received regarding the song and decided to get in touch with a recording studio in Monmouth, South Wales. Up The Lane Studio run by Ron Rogers was delighted to listen to my song and so Susan and I took the 25-minute drive to meet Ron and get his opinion. The place is out in the countryside, quiet, relaxing and welcoming and Ron made me feel comfortable. I explained what I was doing, the concept of the song and what it meant to me but if he thought I was wasting my time he should be open and honest with me. Ron invited me to play the music first without singing which I did and he said very little. Once I'd played it and he had it recorded he took me to another studio downstairs where microphones were set up. He gave me headphones to put on and explained that I would hear what I had just played and then had to sing along to it. This was all so new to me. I had to sing the song three times with instructions that if I make a mistake don't stop just carry on. This I did without any major incident and then went back up to the other studio where Susan had remained. Ron was now at his mixing desk combining the music and the lyrics and overlaying the best parts of my vocals. 'OK,' said Ron, 'now we need some bass.'

He handed me a bass guitar.

'I've never played bass in my life,' I said.

I think he probably knew that already so he just smiled, plugged in the bass and played it along with the sound track. He then added several other instruments from his console and mixing desk and eventually he played the song. Both Susan and myself were blown away by what Ron had achieved. It actually made me sound half-decent. It is amazing what guys like Ron can engineer to sound acceptable! Even though I am from Liverpool, born and bred for the first 21 years of my life, it really is the only thing I can say that I have in common with Lennon & McCartney.

Then Ron dropped a bombshell. 'A CD with only one track isn't much good, what else can you play?'

I wasn't prepared for that. 'Erm… well, as you can see Ron, I'm not much of a musician so I'm limited but I do know the words to the song Africa by Toto (composed by David Paich and Jeff Porcaro) which is appropriate as Kilimanjaro is mentioned.'

Ron went onto his computer. 'OK,' he said, 'we can buy a backing track for that. Come back tomorrow and we'll add your vocals to the track so your CD is a little more appealing.'

I returned to the studio the following day alone as Susan had to go to work. Ron played the backing track and then I went down to the recording studio to add my vocals, again three times. Having completed this I went back up to where Ron was adding the best of the vocals to the track then adding it to my CD and there it was, completed. It sounded reasonable. I have heard some CDs over the years that were by professionals and listening to mine I wasn't put off or discouraged.

I returned home and starting making a few copies along with the insert sleeves for the CDs which I designed and printed with all the necessary accreditations and the words to "Every Step of the Way", just in case somebody wanted to sing along. Susan came home and excitedly asked to hear it. She was pleased with the final result so I sold a CD to her for £5. A good start. I can't say it shot to the top of the national charts but it did hit number 1 in the South Wales' music charts, only because it was the only song in the charts and that was in my mind anyway!

Sales were reasonably brisk mainly to friends and family probably because having heard it they felt sorry for me. However, I did get a few enquiries from elsewhere and was happy to say I sold probably 40 in total. That was £200 and as they say every little helps!

The CD had been a good diversion but I had to get my mind back to training. By now it was late August 2008 and I only had a matter of a few short weeks to complete my preparations and ensure I was as ready as I could be for the challenge.

In the middle of becoming a pop-star, I had received the Itinerary from the organisers including flight details, times and dates. I felt, however, that I didn't want to come straight home, whether or not I had been successful, but rather go and rest somewhere to wind down before getting back into the mundane way of life of work, sleep and cold weather. There was the option of going on Safari to the Serengeti National Park for a week but no, I wanted something more relaxing, sunshine by the Ocean. Only one place for me, Hotel Acajou, Praslin Island, Seychelles. Susan could fly down there and we could meet up at the Hotel. The Acajou is a family-run hotel, managed by Joanise, with an emphasis on being an eco-friendly resort. Susan and I had been to Acajou a couple of years before and had got to know the family and they had become dear friends, as we stayed in constant touch. So, a quick call asking about availability, which I knew wouldn't be a problem, and I made the flight arrangements and cancelled my return flights with the organisers, who weren't too happy with my change of plans. I was to fly from Kilimanjaro Airport to Nairobi, Kenya, then onward directly to Mahe, Seychelles followed by a 15-minute light aircraft flight to Praslin. Susan would fly down directly from UK a couple of days before.

We hadn't originally planned to go to The Seychelles in December 2006 as we wanted to visit Zanzibar but being unable to marry up a flight and a hotel at the same time meant that we had to find an alternative. Our Travel Agent, at the time, suggested The Seychelles and offered us flights and hotel but looking at the hotel online we were not impressed. She suggested that maybe we look at Acajou Hotel, as her final option, which we did and immediately called her back and asked her to book it for Christmas and New Year.

As we discovered on our first visit, The Acajou was all we hoped for as a place to relax and completely wind down. The buildings, rooms, restaurant and bars are mainly constructed from timber which lends itself to a feeling of being at one with nature without taking anything away from the elegant decor in each room. The friendly staff compliment the experience. Standing in its own grounds the hotel is right on the beach so the lapping of the waves, particularly at night, make for a heady cocktail of relaxation and comfort. Standing within the grounds are a number of indigenous Takamaka trees (Calophyllum inophyllum) which, at certain times of the year, provide fruit for the local fruit bat colony. There has been much effort to maintain a 'green' identity to the hotel making it an appealing location to visit, particularly for the growing number of people worldwide who are aware of, and support conservation.

The mission to highlight and utilise local, sustainable materials makes Acajou unique, in addition to its location right on the Cote D'Or Beach, Praslin Island. Needless to say, our stays there have been superb which is one of the reasons we go back and I couldn't think of a more relaxing atmosphere in which to re-coup.

The added significance of the Seychelles was that, as mentioned earlier, it was the only place my father had said he would go abroad if he could. Clearly, there was something that attracted him to those Islands but I didn't know what.

On 23 December 2006, three years exactly to the day that my father, hopefully, was received into the heaven he so longed for all his mortal life, Susan and I waded into the Indian Ocean, flowers in hand, and with love (never a word to be mentioned when I was growing up), threw them into the blue water, with our own, personal individual memories of him.

Upon our return from holiday, I took out my father's war record to see if there could have been any hint that during WW-II that he had come into contact with anybody from the Seychelles. I knew, as I previously mentioned, that he was attached to the Indian Army and I also discovered that about 2,000 Seychellois joined up to the British army to combat the German threat. As much as I have tried, I cannot establish a definitive link but my overwhelming belief is that somebody from the Seychelles was also attached to the Indian army, probably in Italy, with whom my father may have had some contact. It will remain a mystery forever but I do like to think there was a connection, which drew me to those wonderful islands and people.

I was, at this point, getting very excited with this challenge and really couldn't wait to get started but I had to constantly remind myself that whilst it was fraught with possible dangers and hurdles it was Mount Kilimanjaro and was not Mount Everest. I had to get a little perspective into my mind. Anyway, Mount Elbrus, the highest peak in Europe at 5,642 metres (18,510 ft.), Mount Aconcagua, the highest mountain in the Americas at 6,962 metres (22,840 ft.) and Mount Everest, the highest mountain in the world at 8,849 metres (29,031 ft.) could wait, they weren't going anywhere but I had them in my sights. Right now, I wanted to see Kilimanjaro for real instead of just photographs. I wanted to put my foot on the mountain because, as they say, every journey begins with a single step. I was, I felt, ready.

Chapter 4
The Climb

Never give up, never ever, ever give up.
– Winston Churchill

During the week of my scheduled departure, I surprisingly received a number of good luck cards from family and friends. These were unexpected but most welcome, I appreciated them greatly. Even one or two ex-working colleagues had heard about my adventure and sent good luck wishes along with some of Susan's colleagues also. Additionally, I was receiving text messages of good luck, mainly from people in the village and I must admit it buoyed my spirits a lot.

I said my goodbyes to Susan, emotional to say the least, and to Maggie our cat, who would become a great comfort to Susan during the following week. She handed me an envelope as we parted telling me not to open it until I was alone. I took a coach to Heathrow airport, for a pre-arranged meeting with the rest of the team and to get nametags and other instructions, so naturally I opened it en-route. I took out a hand-made card with cut-outs on the front of travel documents, destinations and even a mountain marked "Uhuru" plus a little red button which, when pressed produced a series of flashing lights on the card. Inside it said, *Good Luck, John, I'll be with you,*

EVERY STEP OF THE WAY, with all my love, Susan x and at the bottom an added note (see you in the Seychelles). Very professionally made but also very touching too. I had to remind myself that I was in public and to get a grip of myself.

Due to traffic congestion, I was late and the team had all checked in without me. Luckily, Adrian and I had stayed in touch since our North Wales weekend training trip and he had waited for me near the check-in desk. I was grateful for that but of course this meant that in allocating seats to Nairobi, I was sitting away from the group. An outcast already! Never mind I had enough reading material to keep me occupied and being a seasoned world traveller, it was no problem. I joined the group in the bar for a welcome couple of drinks but never did get my nametag and a couple of other things but did manage to acquire my Alzheimer's Society official T-shirt.

After an uneventful overnight flight, the plane touched down at Jomo Kenyatta International Airport, Nairobi, Kenya and I was able to re-join the rest of the team to embark on our short trip to Kilimanjaro airport on a smaller aircraft.

Jomo Kenyatta was an anti-colonialist politician in Kenya who became the first prime minister in 1963. Then in 1964 he became the first indigenous president, leading the transformation of Kenya from a colony of the British Empire to an independent republic. He was still president until his death in 1978. The country of Kenya is, indeed, indebted to the leadership shown by him, the mantle of which has been taken on as I write this, by his son Uhuru Kenyatta.

We boarded the plane and I was sat with Adrian on one side which turned out to be the wrong side. Shortly before we were due to land at the airport, we flew over Mount Kilimanjaro and those on the opposite side of the plane from us had a clear view of the goal that the successful climbers would reach. Never mind we'd see it soon enough. We were met at Kilimanjaro airport by the organisers from Tanzania and we boarded a coach for the journey to our hotel for the first night, near the municipality of Moshi.

The journey to Moshi would take between 45 and 55 minutes to cover the 40 kilometres (almost 25 miles), and I felt excitement in the air. The landscape was flat, empty and barren with the odd sun-dried plant protruding and little in the way of greenery but completely out of the blue we passed what appeared to be a small settlement with trees and some green vegetation. Many people milled around and I glimpsed what appeared to be market stalls. We passed by quite quickly so it was difficult to take it all in but it was probably an everyday occurrence for residents of what turned out to be the village of Makao Mapya. These small villages became the theme all the way to Moshi and during later investigations I found we had passed by the "Mr Price Market", the villages of Boma Na'dombe and Kwa sadala as well as the "Mnadani live Auction Market" and the "Big Three Market". These kind of places and cultures fascinate me, as they have done in other African countries I have been lucky enough to visit and I wished I had time to go and explore but sadly on this trip it would be impossible.

We arrived in the town of Moshi and more especially at our hotel on the outskirts. Known as the Gateway to Kilimanjaro and the Capital of the Kilimanjaro region with a population of just over 200,000, Moshi has seen trekkers and climbers like us many times. Naturally, we would be welcomed here because that is the kind of people we were now among, not just for the boost to the economy our presence represents but the friendliness and laughter that we received from our hosts.

Moshi is, in fact, one of Tanzania's major coffee-producing areas with many farms also growing maize and beans, as well as there being a very large sugar cane plantation just 20 kilometres away. We would get to see more of the town of Moshi after we had completed our challenge, or not.

Arriving at the hotel we were unable to get a glimpse of the mountain itself as it was surrounded in low cloud so we checked in, with myself and Adrian sharing a room.

As we un-packed we heard a voice outside shouting, 'Look, Kili is clear now. You can see Kili.'

Adrian and I grabbed our cameras and ran out of our ground-floor room and there it was in all its majesty, snow topped, in a pink haze of late afternoon sun, staring down at us, the clouds drifting away as if to say "here is your challenge". We took photographs, many photographs and I stood there emotional, in awe, this is what the last 12 months had been all about. The object of my mind for so many waking hours, and sleeping hours for that matter. Here it was before me. Being the highest freestanding mountain in the world meant that it was totally unmissable, standing out so obvious and not over-shadowed by other mountains, almost out of context with its immediate surroundings. I wondered just how inspiring it was for many people to be living in the shadow of such an imposing prominence.

We were summoned to a group meeting, in the bar, of course, where we were told briefly what to expect over the next five or six days. We knew for instance that some of our party of 24 were not going to make it to the summit that was almost a definite. I just didn't want to be one of those who failed and I felt my determination building up, my enthusiasm almost ready to burst out of me. All I had been through in the previous 12 months were not going to be for nothing. From fund raising and training to dreaming about it and getting over the emotion of the whole experience, I was going to have a go at the highest mountain on the continent of Africa and failure wasn't an option.

We had one or two drinks as well as a delicious meal then it was time to turn in for the night as we had an early wake-up call and breakfast before being transported to the start of our adventure.

Day 1

The following morning Sunday 21 September 2008 we had breakfast, left unwanted luggage at the hotel and boarded the bus to take us to the foot of Mount Kilimanjaro.

We passed several small settlements then ascended into hills. This is where we saw our first coffee-farms. Row upon row of coffee plants with their red berries distinct against the green plants. Harvest time would be just a couple of months away for these Arabica beans and the reward for all the farmers' efforts of growing and nurturing the plants at the start of their journey from the slopes of Kilimanjaro to our coffee cups.

Our route up the mountain would be one of a number of different routes and so we congregated, as designated, at Machame checkpoint to have our documents approved and individual licences signed. As this was being carried out one of our leading organisers suggested we go to a piece of flat grassy ground near the start and carry out some warm-up exercises. We formed a circle and followed our instructor in bending, stretching and running on the spot. There were lots of locals watching us with smiles on their faces as though we were the nearest thing to a circus act. However, it didn't last long as one of our number shouted out, 'Monkey!' There was a Colobus monkey climbing over the fence surrounding the ground we stood on and of course it was far more interesting to go chasing after this wild animal than exercising. Nevertheless, the monkey didn't see it that way and clearly being camera shy, scuttling off into the trees leaving half a dozen disappointed people not quick enough to even get a snapshot.

I wandered around the area taking it all in. People milling around, preparing for their own separate hikes, and I spotted two notice boards giving the rules and points to remember.

1. All hikers should be physically fit.
2. If you experience a sore throat or breathing difficulties do not ascend beyond 3,000 metres A.S.L.
3. Children under 10 are not allowed beyond 3,000 metres A.S.L.
4. If you have heart or lung problems do not attempt the climb without consulting your doctor.
5. Allow plenty of time, ascend slowly.
6. Do not push yourself if your body is exhausted.
7. Drink 4–5 litres of water per day or fruit juice.
8. If symptoms of mountain sickness are apparent you must descend and seek medical treatment.
9. Do not litter the trail; leave it just as you found it.

With all these sensible rules and the need to have licences and insurance it certainly gave an indication how very organised and managed this enterprise was. After all, being a serious source of income for the local area and the local people, it made sense that everything was conducted professionally, limiting the amount of risk that hikers are exposed to and ensuring all possible dangers or problems can be dealt with expeditiously. Other notice boards were on display around the area with more do's and don'ts and I read them all hoping one of them would not say, 'If you're a 57 years old ex-smoker, you ain't gonna do it, mate'!

At around 10.00 am (8.00 am in UK) I was able to get a signal on my mobile phone and call Susan just prior to departing. I later found out that after saying goodbye to me she went into emotional meltdown on the kitchen floor with Maggie in her arms. After gathering herself together she then called her mother who was away in a hotel on holiday. She found out that her mother was having breakfast so asked the receptionist to leave a message saying, 'John is about to start to climb Mount Kilimanjaro.'

The receptionist was, understandably a little baffled by the message, but then realising the situation was only too pleased to pass on the message. Next, Susan telephoned my mother and being Sunday morning, she would be off to church so Susan asked her to say a prayer for my safe return. When she then asked my mum if she wanted her to call her every evening and let her know my progress, Mother declined the offer which was a surprise to Susan. When I found this out, it was, actually, no surprise to me. I'm afraid my family are of the opinion that you don't need to contact each other unless something goes wrong or you need something!

The Machame route is considered to be the most beautiful trail up Mount Kilimanjaro with lots of vegetation and wide panoramic views and so it was to be, certainly for the first day. We would be walking about 10 Kilometres (6.2 miles) in distance and ascending approximately 2,980 metres (9,776 ft.). We would each be carrying our own day sacks containing essentials for each day such as water, chocolate, toiletries and anything else each individual could not do without. Our main baggage such as sleeping bags, spare clothing and the like was carried by the very well organised porters and we would pick up our belongings every evening as we arrived at each overnight camp.

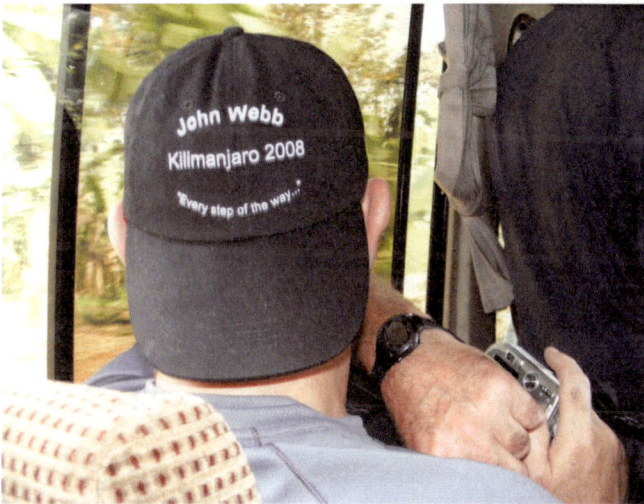

Heading to Mechame Gate

The party started out in high spirits with a lot of excited chattering going on which slowly died away as we ascended. It was a reasonably easy, gradual, climb in the rainforest, interesting and very warm but as we went higher so the temperature cooled a little. We were warned that if it did actually rain the conditions under foot would become very slippery. Fortunately, we didn't experience any rain at all, the going was dry and easy to navigate. We passed many types of plants, some of which are unique to Kilimanjaro such as Dendrosenecio kilimanjari, a giant groundsel which can stand up to five metres in height and Erica arborea not so unique to Kilimanjaro but standing at up to seven meters tall much bigger than in other parts of the world.

Old Man's Beard

There is also a variety of Old Man's Beard (Clematis vitalba) that will only grow in the purest of air. In fact, an area in the far north of Scotland is the only place in the United Kingdom that it can grow. There was also Impatiens kilimanjari or elephant trunk flower. This small, pretty, colourful flower was shaped just like an elephant's trunk thus its name and, obviously, found nowhere else in the world apart from the forest floor of Mount Kilimanjaro.

Impatiens Kilimanjari (Elephant's Trunk)

We stopped at around lunchtime at our designated spot and were greeted by our dining tent and cook tent that had already been erected by the advance party of cooks, guides and porters. Food was served and gratefully accepted but our break for lunch only lasted a short time and off we set again. We emerged from the rainforest to much more open ground and it became apparent quite quickly that there were some stunning views even at this low level.

We had to make it to our first overnight stop at Machame camp. Arriving at around 4.00 pm we were assigned our sleeping quarters with Adrian and I sharing the 2-man tent already set up.

We made a rule that there were to be no boots worn in the tent so we took them off and prepared our sleeping bags before the dark descended upon us. It was so relaxing to be able to discard the dusty boots after so long wearing them and put on soft trainers.

First glimpse of Kili

We had a wander around chatting and relaxing, enquiring as to how everybody had managed so far, and all was well. We were called for dinner and hot food and hot drinks were served up, most welcome after an eight-hour walk. We sat around tables in the dining tent which was in the shape of a football with bright yellow and black pentagonal patches. Easy to see in the event of a whiteout, I supposed. We ate via head torchlight and one or two lamps dotted around. It was very quiet except for our talk until the cooks, guides and porters started singing in their cook tent, which was exactly the same as ours, a yellow and black football. The singing in Swahili was captivating but jolly, with laughter ringing out in between each song. Basically, it went on until it was time for lights out.

After dinner I wandered outside into the pitch black with my telephone but could not get a signal. I did manage to send a text message however, so at least Susan knew I was doing fine. I also sent a text message to Andrew. He wanted to know of my progress so he could update our village website. Susan did not know about this as my texts to him were far more informative than to Susan. Not that there was anything sinister in that but all I wanted Susan to know was everything was positive. In fairness to Andrew, he replied almost immediately with encouraging words.

So far, after day one the weather had been quite kind to us. I had heard stories of just how wet and cold it can be even in Africa at a comparatively low altitude. The day had been largely uneventful but somehow, I knew that would not last. Now it was time for sleep, to rest my body for the more arduous tests ahead over the coming days.

As I trek up that mountain, with you by my side, we can do it to together and you'll be my guide.

Day 2

We were to trek from Machame camp for a little over six hours ascending from 2,980 metres to 3,840 metres (12,598 feet) to Shira camp. However, the ascent was going to be a lot steeper than we had experienced so far. We would be travelling a distance of around nine kilometres (5.6 miles) and walking on the Shira plateau.

I had slept well and was feeling quite lively. Porridge and fresh fruit were served and devoured to get as much energy into our bodies as we could, followed by hot tea and water. Having carried out our personal ablutions we were ready for the next phase.

Uninviting Kili

Arrangements for personal hygiene were well organised. Although there was no question of a hot shower there was plenty of water, some warm, to wash your bits in and brush teeth. Conveniences were portable and set up by the porters and emptied, of course, daily. It was, like most things, a professional set-up and the hygienic answer to a problem all people will have experienced in this kind of situation. We could, in certain places, elect to use the "long-drop" conveniences or pit latrines as they are also known. These were wooden huts with a toilet seat and a hole often located on the side of a cliff and literally whatever you deposit, has a long drop where it is collected and breaks down to eliminate odours, flies and possible diseases. One thing not to forget, of course, is to bring your own toilet paper.

Personally, I found either to be acceptable because, let's face it, you can't hold back nature.

It is, however, one of those topics that some people are reluctant to talk about but it's life, a case of dealing with it in the most hygienic way suitable to each individual.

Susan had been quite organised in packing my change of clothes and had allocated pants, socks shirts for use each day in a separate special waterproof bag, so it was easy for me to ensure I had everything to hand without having to search. I felt very organised.

It was obvious things were getting serious as the gradient became much more severe. Still trekking at this point not actually climbing but able to use walking poles, if anybody required to do so. Personally, I used poles from the start of my training. Anything that helps has to be taken advantage of. Progress was slower than the day before. Again, we stopped at the designated spot around lunchtime and I was amazed to see our cook and dining tents erected as they were when we had left them back at Machame camp, still functioning earlier that morning. I couldn't really work out how they had done that but when we arrived food was already being prepared. Highly efficient guys!

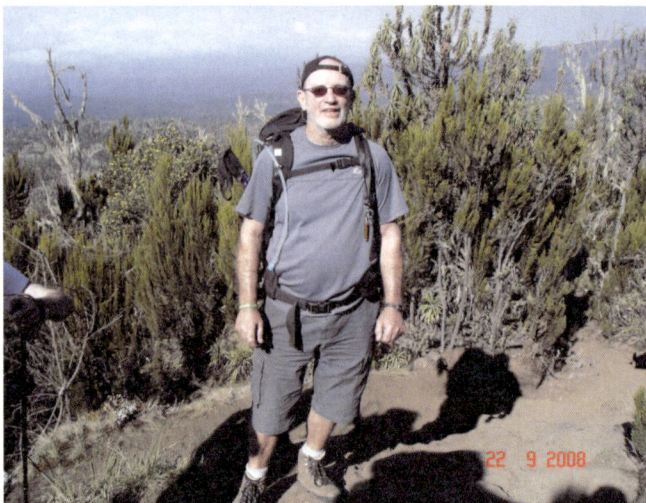

Intrepid Trekker

After lunch we set off again reaching the Shira plateau and as we did so the heavens opened. I looked at my watch, it was 14.30. It rained heavily but fortunately just above the plateau was a cave, to which we all headed and put on our wet weather gear which most of us had already stowed in our daypacks. The temperature had dropped so we didn't waste much time in hanging around as most of us needed a complete change out of wet clothes. A couple of hours later we reached Shira camp and found our luggage and headed to our tents to put on our dry warm clothing.

During that afternoon in particular, I often found myself looking up towards the peak of Kili and was surprised how often the view changed. Not only were the angles different from which to view the summit, only to be expected when on the move, but one minute it was shrouded in heavy mist and the next it was perfectly clear. This continued throughout the rest of daylight time but for me it just added to the mystery that is Kilimanjaro.

Mount Meru in the background

I heard one or two people saying they felt a little rough but nothing serious and hoped it wasn't the start of somebody coming down with the dreaded and feared altitude sickness. We were by this time at about 3,840 metres.

There are three types of altitude sickness, Acute Mountain Sickness (AMS), High-Altitude Pulmonary Edema (HAPE) and High-Altitude Cerebral Edema (HACE).

AMS is the most common when a person ascends to altitudes over 2,500 metres (8,000 ft.) and is caused by the decreasing amount of oxygen available as one gets higher and higher. A trigger for this can be the speed of ascent and the amount of time at that height.

Symptoms include vomiting, nausea, lack of appetite, shortness of breath and insomnia to name but a few. Unless, this is addressed, symptoms will increase and include a persistent cough, fever, continual headache and panting. The longer the condition goes untreated the worse it will get and, in some extreme cases, can result in loss of life.

Treatment is usually descending to a lower altitude immediately and maybe the need for pure oxygen and painkillers.

Prior to making this trip I decided to consult my GP and see if he had any information that he could give me as to how to avoid getting AMS or worse. He pointed out that ibuprofen or paracetamol were good things to have available, and take immediately, should a headache start but, he added, the best way to avoid it is by not climbing too quickly. His advice went like this, 'The younger ones who seem to be in a hurry to get to the top are more likely to contract mountain sickness rather than an old fart who just takes things slowly.'

'Oh, wait a minute,' he added, consulting my medical records, 'you are one of those old farts.' He laughed and I saw the funny side of it too, as he was right!

A Swiss-Ecuadorian extreme speed mountain climber, Karl Egloff, is the holder of the quickest ascent of Kilimanjaro. In 2014 he ascended and descended in an impressive six hours 42 minutes. It would take us six days. As an elite athlete, Karl's body was probably used to fast ascents so he was unaffected by AMS. He holds a number of records for scaling some of the world's most important heights the fastest, such as Mount Aconcagua in Argentina, Mount Elbrus in Russia and Mount Denali in USA to name but a few. Prior to him, in 2010, a Spanish mountain runner, Kilian Jornet, completed the Kilimanjaro trip in seven hours 14 minutes and before that was a Tanzanian guide and mountain runner, Simon Mtuy, who not only trained Kilian Jornet but still holds the record for the quickest, non-supported ascent of Kilimanjaro in nine hours 21 minutes. So, for a few people speed will not hamper their ascent of high peaks and they remain unaffected by mountain sickness but clearly, I was never going to be one of the chosen few.

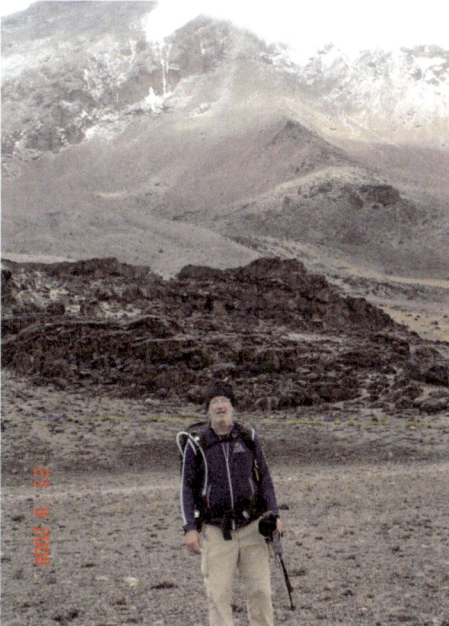

Where am I?

Having reached the overnight camp, we had been joined by a few birds that were identified as white necked ravens (Corvus albicollis). They were quite distinctive being jet black except for the back of the neck being pure white and could be called a little sinister. Generally, adults stand at 50–54 centimetres with a typical wingspan between 75–86 centimetres. They squawked a lot but I think these guys were veterans of stalking trekkers, as they knew just how far to stay away but close enough to remind us that they were there, if we required, should any spare food need to be disposed of.

White Necked Raven

Similarly, one or two of the team were visited by resident rodents at this height, the four-striped mouse (Rhabdomys pumilio). I personally didn't see any but was told one or two tents had been invaded by a couple of them on the hunt for food and probably warmth no doubt.

We had a hot dinner but it was clear there was a problem as two of the party had not wanted to eat and had sought the attention of our travelling doctor.

I wandered out of the dining tent with a couple of the team and looked into the night sky which was free from light pollution. This was probably my first real experience of dark sky with the number of stars almost beyond comprehension. I had never knowingly seen the night sky quite like that. Then suddenly a shooting start was visible. Fantastic! Then one of the guys in possession of a GPS device said in two minutes you'll be able to see the International Space Station and sure enough it appeared with cries of "wow there it is", as it moved across the blackness dotted with millions of stars. Then another shooting star. Awesome!

Looking cold

In due course, I went to bed leaving Adrian and a couple of the others in the dining tent playing cards, I read a while, made some notes in my diary and that was it. I didn't hear Adrian come into the tent, I was dead to the world.

I know you'll protect me, with your arm around my soul. I can't do it on my own, but with you I'm not alone.

With my brothers

Day 3

I woke early on day three and immediately became aware that I was warm but the air was very, very cold. Andrew had given me lots of advice prior to the trip, of which one of the most valuable was, to buy a top-quality sleeping bag that would keep me warm all night enabling me to sleep. He pointed out that if I was cold at night I wouldn't sleep and if I didn't sleep, I wouldn't have the energy to successfully finish the climb. It was sound advice and that's just what I did shelling out over £600. It was worth the expense. I slept very well each and every night, never feeling cold and certainly rejuvenated each morning. I was aware of one or two of the party had not taken this into account and not having slept soundly, had suffered as a result.

Overnight, a couple of the team had been overcome with mountain sickness and as soon as possible had been taken off the mountain or, at least, to a camp at a lower level. I think at this point we were down by two people so far but it was obvious others were on the brink.

After the rain of the previous day one or two trekkers had left their wet clothes outside with the intention of drying them. However, the plummeting temperature overnight had just made them rigid with ice. Trousers could actually stand up by themselves.

Today would be tough. We were to climb from our current 3,840 metres up to 4,630 metres (15,190 ft.) then down to 3,950 metres (12,959 ft.) and should take around seven hours in all. Apart from this being the natural route we were following, climbing to a higher level then descending to a lower one is helpful in acclimatising. I had read that on some climbs a part of the strategy is to climb high and sleep low. This is what we will do today. We were to go up the Shira Route via the Moir Hut Camp and the Northern Circuit, through Sharks Tooth to Lava Tower Camp. Sharks Tooth was a point where Porters could shortcut the climb without having to go all the way up to the Lava Tower and down the other side. The Lava Tower is a tower that was formed by volcanic activity over 150,000 years ago when Kilimanjaro was still a triple volcano. Volcanic matter spewed out of the erupting mountain and created the 90-metre tower. It gives a fascinating 360-degree view of the environment and is popular with climbers.

On this particular day, however, one of our numbers would also take the shortcut at the Sharks Tooth with the porters due to not feeling well and eventually, sadly, would be escorted down the mountain unable to complete the climb.

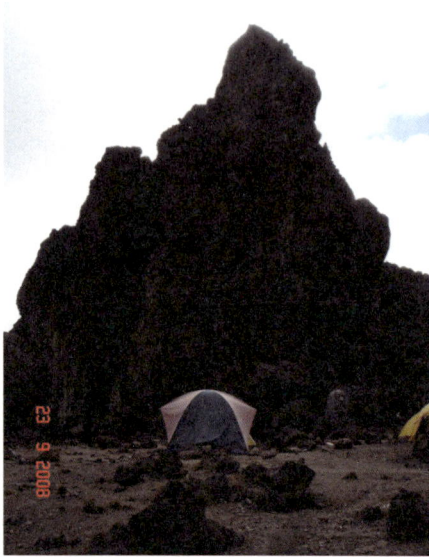

The Lava Tower

We would descend down from the Lava Tower to the Barranco Camp for our stay overnight.

It was a very bright and clear morning and I looked around me in the distance when my eyes became fixed on another mountain seemingly not far away. I enquired about this mountain that looked just a little lower than Kilimanjaro and was informed it was Mount Meru, sister mountain of Kili and in fact, about 70 kilometres (45.5 miles) from us in the Arusha Region. I swear it looked a lot closer than that. Mount Meru stands at 4,562 metres (14,967 ft.) and is the fifth highest in Africa.

It was first ascended in 1904 but it erupted in 1910, considerably more recent than Kilimanjaro. It is now classed as an active but dormant stratovolcano, meaning that it is built up of layers (strata) of lava and ash. Many people see it as being a "warm-up" climb before tackling Kilimanjaro while others feel it is its own unique challenge and unfair to treat it as a practice obstacle.

After ablutions we breakfasted, getting as much porridge and fresh fruit we could to boost energy levels as well as plenty of hot tea and anything else each individual could get to keep them going. Chocolate was a favourite. We then prepared to move off.

So far so good

The going was quite hard at first, at least for me, but soon I was in my stride, slow and purposeful remembering what my doctor had told me about young men and old farts.

During the day as we neared the Lava Tower, I picked up two pieces of stone. The first was black and shiny and one of the guides identified it as Obsidian. I'd never heard of it before but research since has led me to discover that Obsidian is a naturally occurring volcanic glass extruded from a volcano and cools to a hard substance and is an igneous rock. It actually comes from felsic lava and contains elements such as silicon, oxygen, aluminium and potassium. It is not exclusive to Africa however, and can be found in many parts of the world. Obsidian became very useful for making weapons such as spears, arrowheads and knives and tools for agriculture due to its sharpness, smoothness and hardness. It is a fact, that even today Obsidian is used for certain surgical procedures due to its natural sharpness and can produce a much finer scalpel blade than conventional steel. It is also said to aid wound healing and scar superiority after surgery quicker, due to the properties in the volcanic glass.

The second stone I picked up was pumice. Again, pumice is an igneous rock but very rough textured. I'd heard of pumice years ago as it was a permanent fixture in the bathroom of my grandparents. It is created when super-heated, highly pressurised rock is violently ejected from an erupting volcano. It is light in colour and highly porous but it has a very low specific gravity and has the ability to float on water. Large deposits of pumice are used in construction and when mixed with other concrete products, produce a lighter building block with higher insulation than standard blocks. Pumice is also used in landscaping and horticulture for decoration and drainage. Furthermore, pumice is used in soaps, pencil erasers, skin exfoliating, polishing and many other everyday uses. Certainly, pumice seems to be quite versatile even in our modern-day society.

We lunched just below the Lava Tower taking on board as much nutrition as we could then, filling our water bottles or platypus's we continued passing the tower and began our decent along the Umbwe Route and to Barranco Camp. A platypus is a watertight bag with a tube coming from it which fits inside your day sack or rucksack. The tube, with a valve on the end, is available to intake water whenever you wish rather than having to stop and take a bottle from your bag.

During the day I realised that certain things were passing me by, literally. I took for granted that at each stop for lunch or overnight our cook tent and dining tent would be erected and functioning by the time we arrived as well as our sleeping tents and luggage. So, I took more notice of what was happening around me. As I was climbing, I was constantly overtaken by porters, not only carrying, what turned out to be our overnight bags but the tents themselves, the tables, chairs and food, as well as fetching fresh water en route daily. These guys were working phenomenally hard. At one stage I noticed a porter carry a large inverted table on his head with three full trays of fresh eggs strapped to his back. Total respect for the whole team!

Even more respect when I discovered they were paid between US$1 and US$9 per day depending on their rank. I also found out that they came from all over Tanzania in the hope of being selected and trained to, eventually, be a guide which is a very prestigious position to hold.

Looking up towards the summit I was taken by the change in the landscape above us. Nothing green appeared but everything was grey, cold and very uninviting. We seemed to be far below the summit and yet I knew we were closer to the top than the bottom. The snow line appeared to confirm that was the case and in a way it kind of deflated me for a short while but ever the optimist I just carried on to the next camp.

Later, I got to chatting with Oscar, my guide, and another guide, Justice. Both had so much experience climbing in the area, as well as conducting safaris on the Serengeti. They had been up and down this mountain so many times they knew virtually every footstep and each individual route. We talked about the mountain, the changeable weather, how often they summited, going on safari and things like that but the one, unrelated subject we touched on was football. I knew that in Tanzania, like many African countries, football and in particular English Premier League was very popular, attracting many to the television screens. I learned that both of the guys were fervent Liverpool Football Club fans. As it so happened, I had brought along with me two Liverpool football shirts, with the purpose of perhaps giving them to somebody who demonstrated a bias towards my club. These two guys were perfect. I went to my tent and pulled out the two shirts, unsure if they would fit these two tall men. No sooner had I handed them over than they were wearing them and, along with Adrian, we gave a rendition of the Liverpool Anthem "You'll Never Walk Alone", for all and sundry to enjoy! Giving those shirts seems to form an immediate bond between us and they were absolutely thrilled to be the new owners of such famous club shirts. Between the two of them they were to look after me for the rest of the climb.

We drank hot tea as we waited for dinner to be served and I remember thinking that I was really happy as to how I was feeling. I was in good shape, although I knew the hardest part was yet to come but nevertheless, I was content that it was so far so good. However, I also knew that unlike some of my younger travelling companions I would be hitting the hay earlier rather than later after dinner. Preservation of my body was important.

We ate all together in the dining tent with much chatter going on and, of course, laughter but we were aware that tomorrow was going to be a long and arduous day.

I disappeared to bed, quickly followed by Adrian. I don't think many would be staying up too late tonight. I read a while by torchlight and then made some notes of the day's events in my diary. The diary was becoming important to me as I built up a picture of daily life on the mountain. Inevitably, in the mists of time, certain details would be lost and I was anxious to record as much as I could. Sadly, however, as I write this from memory, the diary is lost.

In my mind, unplanned, in my solitary moments, I had the embryo of another song. Where it came from, I don't know but during my note taking each evening I was adding to it. Just words, at this stage without any kind of tune or melody but I was slowly piecing it together. Maybe the elevation was addling my brain and making me think I was a songwriter, I don't know but I was just writing down what came to my mind. Probably wouldn't go anywhere anyway.

I slid down into my warm bag and quickly fell asleep.

On the top of that mountain, I'll be closer to you. Let me feel that you're beside me and that love is here too.

Day 4

Overnight drama meant that another two of our team would not be summiting, sadly for them. Mountain sickness had affected one whilst the other had experienced a fall the previous day and damaged her back. She was unable to walk without pain and climbing was out of the question. She was guided down the mountain in pain and, no doubt, extremely disappointed.

As usual, we breakfasted and prepared for this day that would be hard, with reduced sleep, due to our schedule. We set off from Barranco Camp and were immediately confronted with the Barranco Wall, a cliff like structure rising 257 metres (843 ft.) and looking very ominous. It actually isn't technically a difficult climb as there are many handholds and footholds but it is best to put away your trekking poles, if using, and rely on your physical fitness and judgement to get to the top of this steep cliff. Taking it slowly is the key making sure each foothold and handhold is secure. Nicknamed the "Barranco Breakfast Wall" it is the first thing you do after breakfast on this particular route, and it took me a little over an hour to climb, although I must confess it seemed a lot longer.

At the top of the Barranco Wall the path, called The Southern Circuit, leads to the Karanga Valley whcre the Karanga Camp is found. We, however, were not going to stop at this camp; our plan was to continue on until lunchtime. After lunch, our schedule meant that we would have a 3-hour climb to Barafu Camp at 4,550 metres (14,924 ft.).

We embarked on the final climb for the day along the Mweka Route which was a hard, very steep incline. The landscape was extremely void of any vegetation and we were just below the snow line climbing ever so closer to it and feeling the cold much more. At one point the cloud cleared and Mount Meru appeared again in the distance. I looked up to the summit of Kilimanjaro bathed in bright sunlight and strangely enough it appeared to be further away than it had a couple of hours before. I'm sure it was just an illusion or my eyes playing games. Then, as happens on Kilimanjaro, again, the clouds swallowed up the summit and the sun also disappeared leaving us in a half-light in mid-afternoon.

Arriving at Barafu Camp, it had been as hard as I anticipated but I was glad, I had made it feeling in decent condition with no sign of mountain sickness at all. Lashings of tea were on offer prior to dinner but we were all due for an early night as we would be starting the following day at midnight so it was important to grab as much sleep as possible.

After an early dinner it was basically straight to bed, for about 4 hours of much needed shut-eye. We would be woken at 11.00 pm to give us an hour to prepare for the final push to the top. 11.00 pm came about 10 minutes later or so it seemed. Both myself and Adrian were up, dressed, ready and enthusiastic, sort of. The best part of it was we were both feeling good, unaffected either by the height or fatigue and we downed porridge, tea, water and chocolate and prepared ourselves ready for whatever it was that lay ahead.

'Drink as much water as you can,' we were advised. 'If it gets that cold at the summit your water will be most likely be frozen so undrinkable,' we were told.

When we reach the top we'll stand, looking down upon that land. I'll be happy on that day, Every Step of the Way.

Day 5

Midnight arrived and off we went on the dot. Each trekker had a guide close at hand and, of course, I had Oscar with me. Slowly, we walked into the blackness and I looked up on occasion to see headlights bobbing up and down higher up the mountain, as some other teams had set out earlier than we had. Most of us were quiet. I was, for a while at least, keeping my own council, preparing mentally for what I was about to do. Keeping in my head, that I cannot give up, no matter how hard it becomes and that right now is what the last 12 months had been all about, it was this time, this moment, this next seven hours that were to be the most important in all that year.

I was thinking also of my dad, Grandad, Uncle Bill and those who I didn't know but whose photographs I had secreted in my pocket. Thinking what they had gone through having been struck down by the abhorrent Alzheimer's disease, ruining and changing lives forever. I was doing this to help research into the disease, in my small way, to help find, if not a cure, maybe an improvement in treatment that will prolong life with quality rather than reducing the life span of sufferers and affording them absolutely no dignity whatsoever. Alzheimer's and indeed all dementia conditions did this to people, cruelly, unpredictably and savagely.

Getting colder

The climb was steep, that's for sure, and I was going slow but purposefully trying not to look up but concentrating on my footsteps in my head torch. I noticed that as we slowly ascended it was becoming a lot colder and my breathing was becoming heavier.

Words of encouragement were uttered by various people in the party with the most common being "Pole, Pole" in Swahili meaning "Slowly, Slowly" it was the only way to be successful taking our time. I, on the other hand had no choice. It was going to be either Pole, Pole or stop!

During the week, I had picked up one or two Swahili words, with the help of Oscar. For instance, Jambo means hello, Jambo Bwana means hello sir, Astante is thank you, karibou means welcome and appropriately for where we heading, Uhuru means freedom. Hakuna Matata was already known amongst many as it had been frequently used in the 1994 Disney film; The Lion King so many knew it meant take it easy or no trouble. Well, that was about the limit of my Swahili and I concentrated on these words as we climbed to take my mind off the more strenuous effort I had having to exert as we got higher.

After, I suppose, a couple of hours, I realised that every so often there seemed to be a raised hump in the ground. Maybe every couple of hundred metres we would have to negotiate these and the higher we got the more difficult I was finding it to climb over. I estimated that each hump was probably less than a metre high but the effort required was getting more and more, or the humps were getting bigger and bigger, I couldn't work out which it was. I was tiring and I knew that, but kept gulping water from my platypus tube, while I could, which helped me to stay focussed.

I wasn't saying much to anybody just following Oscar with Adrian behind me. Then maybe after about four and a half hours my breathing was becoming laboured and I had slowed so much.

Adrian lost patience with me. I'm not sure if he was suffering with a little bit of altitude sickness but he shouted, 'John, you're going to slow, I'm getting cold.'

'Well carry on, mate,' I replied, 'overtake me and get going and I'll see you at the top,' not really knowing if I was going to make it in truth.

We continued up. Me following Oscar looking down at his heels when suddenly I became transfixed. Instead of seeing his heels I saw all manner of colours and all kinds of shapes where his heels had previously been, although they were still there, I knew that, deep in my muddled mind. It was almost as if I was staring down the barrel of a kaleidoscope seeing all these shining, colourful objects before my eyes. I was hallucinating that is for sure. Over another hump and down the other side jogged me from my trance and I stopped. Oscar stopped. It was quiet and I was breathing heavily.

'I can't do this anymore, Oscar,' I said, 'I really need to rest a while.'

'No, John, you can't rest,' he replied, 'it's too cold.'

'But my energy levels have gone, Oscar, and I can't breathe, I'm sorry.'

'John, my brother, it's not far now, you can make it' was his reply.

I looked up and saw numerous headlamps that seemed to be quite high up the mountain.

'Oscar, you're a bloody liar,' I replied and we both laughed.

'Not as far as you think, my brother,' he said, putting his hand on my shoulder reassuringly.

For that short time, a minute, maybe two, I shocked myself. The mere thought of defeat? I'd never seriously contemplated failure before and here I was not far from the summit doubting myself. How could I let down those I was doing this for? Not just those affected by Alzheimer's but those who had given support in so many ways, Susan, Andrew, the villagers, my mum, Susan's mum to mention just a few. No, I told myself, this was not going to beat me, 'come on you old fart, get going.'

Then, without warning, the adage of the late Sir Winston Churchill hit me. 'Never give up, never ever, ever give up.' It was like a ton of bricks dropping onto my head, only to confirm that there was no other option and that success was just up that hill!

So, with every gram of my energy, with every fibre of my being I pushed on, my fingers and toes becoming numb with cold and I just followed Oscar.

Summit night

It was the injection of belief in myself I needed, I think, the encouragement from Oscar and the stern bollocking I gave myself that enabled me to very quickly banish any thought of giving up although I must confess, I was, and I knew it, struggling badly both with fatigue, which seemed to have hit me rather quickly, and my breathing. I kept thinking why the hell did I take up smoking all those years before? Idiot!

We continued the ascent with Oscar periodically checking to see if I was OK or ensuring I was still there, I don't know which but probably both.

'Keep the doctor away from me Oscar and keep me away from the doc,' I pleaded, knowing that it was likely if she saw me and how I was struggling she probably would order me off the mountain and that just wasn't going to happen, not now, it couldn't, could it?

I remember concentrating a lot on putting one foot in front of the other, head down, purposefully, with my mind all over the place but then became aware of a strange taste in my mouth. Suddenly I realised.

The unmistakable taste of blood! Where had it come from? Internally? That was a bit worrying. I stopped momentarily and spat onto the floor and in my headlight, I confirmed, indeed, it was blood. *Damn and blast*, I thought, *what's happened?* I rubbed my tongue across my bottom lip and immediately felt relief. I'd bitten my bottom lip. It was swollen and bloody so I took a tissue from my pocket dabbed it a little but it continued to bleed although a little less now. I held the tissue over my mouth, making it even more difficult to breath, and squeezed my lip for a minute. It seemed to do the trick and stopped the bleeding. Oscar was concerned and kept enquiring if I was OK but I was able to re-assure him everything was fine, with half the tissue bonded by blood to my wound, and my lip feeling three times its normal size as I spoke.

I assumed there was one or two of the team slightly ahead of us, with Adrian having disappeared into the blackness earlier and so I just called out, 'Has anyone seen the doctor?'

'No,' came the reply, much to my relief.

I was feeling a little more enthusiastic by now after about six hours almost non-stop climbing and walking. I even had a second wind and my energy level crept back up, slightly, helped, I think by the fact that dawn was breaking over the mountain, it was getting light, it was as if I'd been reborn into a new world and I could see all around me. It seemed to happen very quickly or maybe in my state of mind I imagined it. The sun shone with not a cloud above us but it was bitterly cold. My thermometer was fixed on -5C but a little breeze probably made it feel colder taking into account the wind-chill factor.

Made it. When we reach the top we'll stand

'Stella Point,' said Oscar, 'we are almost at Stella Point.'

Stellar Point is 5,756 metres (18,885 ft.) and considered to be one of three summits on Kilimanjaro. A climber choosing not to go any further will indeed be awarded their certificate for climbing Kili.

I already knew reaching Stella Point, for some, was an achievement and considered a success and I also understood and respect the reasons why people would not wish to go any further due to perhaps, fatigue, AMS or just content to attain this level. Oscar suggested that maybe I consider it. I refuse to commit in writing my reply to him but it made him laugh loud! After all, we were standing at 5,756 metres and Uhuru Point, the actual summit, was only 139 metres higher albeit that it takes another 30 to 45 minutes at least, to get there.

The crater – home to some special photos

We skirted the crater on which Stellar Point is situated and continued our ascent. Rounding the rocks to our left the crater to our right we suddenly, unexpectedly saw in the distance the summit. Uhuru Peak was in touching distance. I could see some people milling around the sign at the final destination, pretty soon I'd be joining them. It really was a shot in the arm for my confidence.

An ice field

The path from the crater to Uhuru was only a slight gradient not a hard climb more and stiff walk and very dry and dusty but to our left we passed huge ice fields meters high. These were the permanent snows of Kilimanjaro, made famous in a short story by Ernest Hemingway in 1936 and subsequently an Oscar nominated film in 1952. It was a privilege to be so close to them. We reached the immediate area around Uhuru and there was Adrian and George and several others from the team.

'Well done, John, you did well,' said George. 'Even I found this climb difficult,' he added. George had summited Kili on several occasions but this he said was the hardest ever and he couldn't explain why.

Adrian and I shook hands congratulating each other on our success and I approached the sign and looked up.

CONGRATULATIONS YOU ARE NOW AT UHURU PEAK TANZANIA, 5,895M AMSL, Africa's Highest Point, The World's Highest Free-Standing Mountain.

The emotion was immense, emotion I never knew I was capable of feeling, I never knew it was in me. So, many clichés can be used to describe how I felt but relief, pride, delight, happy, successful achievement, are all thoughts that ran through my mind. Adrian grabbed my camera and started snapping pics of me alone at the signpost, my cleaned-up swollen lip just about visible, a battle scar, I guess. Then somebody took over the camera and Adrian joined me for a few pictures.

These were joyous moments which I was determined to take advantage of, to enjoy and most of all to remember but they were to be short lived as Oscar reminded me that we can't stay too long due to the temperature. I understood, as inactivity brings on cold and tiredness very quickly.

I took the opportunity of stepping away from the group and walked to the side of the large Kibo crater, and peered into that grey, snow flaked chasm. Reaching into my pocket I pulled out a small container. In it were copies of the photographs that I'd had on display at the auction of all the people I now knew of who had been affected by Alzheimer's disease, people who I had highlighted in the build-up to this climb. I had also added a photograph of Susan's father, Ivor, who lost his battle with cancer in 2000 but I felt it appropriate to add him because I know he would have been my biggest supporter in this quest had he been still with us. I held the container in my hand, thought about my dad and whispered, 'This is for you' and threw it into the crater shouting, 'Every

Step of the Way.' So emotional and so meaningful in that moment, for me. I hid my tears with difficulty. *Don't cry, John*, I thought, *your tears might just freeze on your face and you look bad enough already.*

I returned to the group who had by now dispersed somewhat and picked up my rucksack, threw it on and I followed Oscar and Adrian back to Stellar Point.

I had done it! My task complete, my aim achieved. Put in any, or in every other way possible I didn't let myself down and more especially didn't let my dad down, my grandad, my uncle and all the other people. It was, in fact, taking a while to really sink in. Maybe to some, climbing Kilimanjaro was nowhere near as difficult as others, more arduous treks people undertake in the name of adventure or challenge, but for me personally it was massive and I felt so thankful I had completed it.

My breathing was still troubling me and George asked if I was OK but I laughed it off with the old ex-smoker excuse and started going down the way we had come up in the dark. It really didn't feel like the same place.

Trying to get a message to Susan to tell her I'd made it was impossible. No signal wherever I stood as had been the case throughout the week. I had only been able to send text messages of re-assurance to her but was so disappointed not to have been able to tell her myself of my success directly. I explained to Adrian who was luckier with his telephone and was able to contact his wife, Shirley, to tell her he had made it. He then asked Shirley to call Susan to tell her I'd made it too.

I found out eventually that Susan had spent the night in bed with Maggie, who is not normally allowed in or on the bed, and had not slept well, worrying about me. When she got the call from Shirley she broke down in tears with relief, after all she had lived the whole experience with me for the past 12 months and was elated it had ended in success but she too, like me, was frustrated that we couldn't speak and hadn't spoken since day one when we were about to set off from Machame Gate.

I had all this time been in constant touch with Andrew by text messages, unknown to Susan, and had given him much more detailed information, explaining how tough at times I found it but my last and most important message was that I'd made it! In fairness to Andrew, he had returned my messages quickly and was obviously delighted that it had been a success.

Susan explained at a later point that she left for work that morning she opened her car windows as she cruised through the village with "Every Step of the Way" blasting from her CD player. I'm fairly sure some would have heard it and got the message!

We were to return to our previous camp, Barafu, which was a 3-hour walk; to pick up anything we had left behind there the night before as travelling light had been the most advantageous way to conquer the summit. We had an hour at Barafu to collect our belongings, have a cup of tea and a snack then join the Mweka Route for a 2-hour descent to our final overnight stop, Millennium Camp. It was only while we were at Barafu that I was aware that we had lost a couple of the team overnight, due to mountain sickness. In all, of the 24 people who started this Trek, 17 had been successful. This must have been bitterly disappointing for the other seven to say the least because for me I know it would have been completely soul destroying. I can only hope those who did not make it to the summit found consolation in knowing they did raise money for Alzheimer's Society and that it would be put to very good use in care or research to help overcome this dreadful disease.

I began to realise that this whole endeavour had set off a change in me as a person, even at 57 years of age. To change as an individual it is clear, you have to be in an uncomfortable situation, whether by design or accident, to understand just what you really are capable of. It makes sense when you think about it.

However, my breathing was still causing me difficulties. Reluctantly, I sought out our travelling lady doctor and explained my problem.

'Shirt off,' she said, 'let's have a listen to that chest.'

I stripped down to my shirt and lifted it up, too cold on the side of the mountain to go topless. She examined my chest and back with her stethoscope and tapped with her fingers as I wheezed in deep breaths when told.

'You need a course of steroids,' she pointed out and went to her drug supplies. 'Take 10 of these tablets now, 9 tomorrow, 8 the day after and so forth until you finished them all,' she instructed and handed me the packs of little white pills. 'You should also use an inhaler for a couple of days as and when you need it,' she added, handing me a blue inhaler which I discovered was called Ventolin commonly used for breathing difficulties as I was experiencing. She explained how to use it as I had never come into contact with these before.

'So, you think I have asthma?' I asked. 'Probably not but you might be borderline COPD (Chronic obstructive pulmonary disease),' which she explained was not uncommon in smokers and ex-smokers.

She advised that I visit my general practitioner on my return to UK but was fairly sure that the medicines she had given me would bring relief fairly quickly. I thanked her so much, got dressed as I was starting to feel the cold and went to take the first of my pills.

Oscar and I started down with most of the team already on their way. Knowing we had a 2-hour descent made me not wish to hurry and Oscar too was happy with that. Adrian went ahead, I'll see him at the final Camp.

The route down was quite tricky. Loose scree almost made it like a ski slope and I did slide around on occasion. Oscar insisted he take my rucksack so I wouldn't be overbalanced and although I didn't want to, ("never give up, never ever, ever give up" came to mind), I took the sensible option and handed him my sack.

As we continued our way down, I heard footsteps behind me. Purposeful, regimented, more than one set of steps I turned around to see two burly looking guys, clearly mountain guides, carrying another guy between them. His feet weren't even touching the ground and his head pointed upwards to the sky as though unconscious. Oscar called out, in Swahili naturally to them as they passed, so I didn't understand and they replied. Apparently, the guy has serious mountain sickness and they are getting him off the mountain and to a medical facility with utmost urgency.

'It looks serious,' he said.

'I hope he is OK,' I replied.

'He's a Frenchman,' Oscar added, nonchalantly.

We carried on our way down and amidst the scree and shale was a flat dugout area where I could see something but couldn't make out what it was. Curious, I diverted over to it. There was a folded metal and wire contraption and I studied it for a minute before Oscar followed me over and enlightened me.

'It's a stretcher,' he said, 'an emergency stretcher, just in case somebody cannot be carried by the guides.'

The first thing that struck me was that it looked incredibly uncomfortable but then again if you so bad you can't walk, would you care anyway? If memory serves me right Oscar pointed out there are a number of them around the mountain and had been donated by various organisations such as the International Red Cross.

The scree and stones were hard work and during one of my slips I caught my foot on one of the sharp stones. In some parts they were as sharp as razors and as I slipped, some of the stones ripped my boot. It never touched my foot but made a small gash in one of my treasured boots, the boots I was so grateful for from Andrew. I was dismayed about this but, whilst it wasn't uncomfortable and caused no injury, I couldn't do anything about it then so I would have to deal with it later. At least it wasn't raining or wet under foot.

Eventually, we left the scree and found ourselves on a more conventional path. A lot easier to negotiate and I took my rucksack from Oscar... only wimps have people carry their baggage.

We arrived at Millennium Camp by now mid-afternoon. Most of the team were sat on benches drinking bottles of beer, Kilimanjaro Premium Lager or the other favourite, Serengeti Premium Lager. A huge cheer went up when I arrived in camp with several of the guys wanting to buy me a bottle for which I was so grateful. I glugged the first mouthful down. Nectar no doubt about it, cold amber nectar. Absolutely delicious. I sat down with the guys as most of them said, well done, the old man had made it. I do rather think many of them thought I wouldn't successfully summit the mountain just by the way they greeted me and said, well done.

They didn't really know me. Although my breathing was giving me concern other than that I was feeling good, tired, of course but who wouldn't be after a 7-hour ascent followed by a 5-hour descent with only one hour to rest.

The bottle of beer was quickly followed by one or two others and at that point I was more than happy but, like us all, I needed food. I did wonder if the beer would have any adverse effect with the steroids the doctor had given me but to be honest that thought lasted about two seconds as the beer was so nice and anyway, I didn't actually care at that point.

As had been the case throughout the week the tents were erected the cook tent and dining tent were also erected and cooking was under way. A band of, mainly happy, trekkers tucked into hot food, tea and fruit. I felt fairly sure most people felt similar to me, knackered particularly after a couple of drinks and food. Looking back now I cannot even remember what time it was but I know it was dark and my sleeping bag was calling me, loud and persistent!

Susan later told me that the night after I had summited, she and Andrew met up for a celebratory drink at The Woodlands Tavern and as she ran down the lane to meet Andrew she shouted, 'He did it,' to which Andrew replied, 'I know,' much to Susan's surprise and somewhat disappointment. He then confessed that we had been in close touch throughout the trip and he was also able to give her more information than I had told her about.

Sleep was to come very easy to me that night but before that I enthusiastically wrote in my diary that I'd made it! This was my final night on the mountain but in a strange way I didn't want it to end. I finished writing, switched off my head torch and just lay in the blackness with a warm feeling of satisfaction washing over me as I drifted into another world.

Every Step of the Way, be it night or be it day. Whatever I have to do, I'll do it for you.

Day 6

I had rested well and felt refreshed the following morning although aware that my breathing was still very wheezy. I took a gulp of the inhaler, Ventolin, which slightly eased it but I needed to pop the next nine pills of my course. Adrian and I were up and dressed both ravenous and went to the dining tent. I grabbed some water and washed down my tablets in case I forgot later, then it was into the porridge and fruit again. I was, however, getting a little fed up with porridge but it had been a necessity these past days. I longed for full English. The thought of bacon, eggs, sausages, black pudding and baked beans with hot toast or fried bread made my mouth salivate until the next spoonful of porridge brought me back to earth!

Just prior to putting on my boots I decided to inspect the damage caused by the scree the day before. The slash in the leather was worse than I thought. I did wonder if I could have them repaired on my return home. Then I had a thought. I found Oscar and asked him if he thought the boot could be repaired locally. He confirmed that yes it could be and make it water tight again.

'OK,' I said, 'are there any of your colleagues who these boots might fit?'

Without a word he disappeared and returned with a young guy probably my height who was wearing a really tatty pair of soft boots.

'This guy is in need of new boots,' Oscar said. 'If he doesn't get them, he won't be able to be a guide,' he added. 'Can he get them repaired?' I asked. Oscar spoke to him in Swahili.

'Yes, my brother,' Oscar replied, 'he can.'

'OK,' I said, 'tell him to find me at the bottom and he can have them,' I said.

Oscar relayed my offer. The guy's face lit up and he grabbed me by the hand and shook it vigorously.

'Thank you, Bwana, thank you so much,' he said. Smiles all round.

'He'll be able to carry on and become a guide now,' Oscar added.

I was glad I'd taken that decision and I felt sure Andrew would have been in full agreement.

After breakfast and ablutions, we had to pack up our belongings for one final time on the mountain. This was done in a great atmosphere on that morning in camp and then we were summoned to a point where the cooking staff, porters, guides, all of our hosts, had gathered. We stood in a long line facing them not knowing what was coming next. It was a clear morning, bright, sunny with a blue cloudless sky and as I looked across to them, I was aware that in the background

Kilimanjaro was looking down on us majestically, the snow-capped summit glistening as though it was saying, 'Well done old man, you conquered me!'

Without warning, one of their number who turned out to be a sort of choirmaster, started singing "Jambo, Jambo Bwana". Pretty quickly the rest of the group joined in and gave us a rendition, clearly practised, but done in great spirits and delivered with fun, laughter, clapping and dancing. Next up was another Swahili song which I must confess I didn't understand except it was, naturally, about Kilimanjaro. Nevertheless, it was great fun to watch, clap along with and laugh too. I was standing with an insulated mug of tea in one hand and my camera in the other, enjoying this occasion, when suddenly out of the crowd opposite came one of the guys with whom I was unfamiliar. Dancing his way across the void between us, he headed for me, grabbing me by the hand and dragging me into the no man's land between us. He danced as everybody was, and I, in my way, joined in, breathless, laughing, holding on to my mug of tea and camera. The whooping and the hollering reached a crescendo at this point as I danced and was joined by the perpetrators of this set up, Oscar and Justice as I wheezed my way around on that dry dusty ground. I felt privileged they had singled me out, even though I was coughing and gasping somewhat. I guess the old man made an impression somewhere along the route. After a few minutes I returned to my place with the team laughing and happy, trying desperately to get my breath back. We were regaled with a third song from our hosts with everybody in high spirits as they walked in file across to us, still singing, and went down the line shaking hands, bumping fists thanking each other and in some cases hugging. What a wonderful way to finish this adventure. When different worlds come together everybody can benefit, one way or the other. Sharing cultures can only be a positive thing, making friends, priceless.

That dance

After my return to UK and completely out of the blue, I was sent a recording of the whole event of that entertaining time. I was highly delighted and grateful to receive it and even happier to be able to show Susan and many friends and family, who for that short time, were able to live a little of it with me. That recording is so precious to me, I do watch it from time to time usually with a smile on my face and always dancing along but now, with more breath!

We had a 16 kilometres (9.94 miles) descent to complete which would take between four to five hours until we reached the finish at Mweka Gate. It was still early morning and so after retrieving our belongings packed into day sacks, stocked up on fresh water we set off in dribs and drabs. The final trek was not at all stressful as we descended back into rainforest. A cloud free morning continued as we walked through green vegetation along a designated path.

Back in the rainforest

High above me at one point a couple of Colobus monkeys played in the trees but apart from that there were no signs of wild life.

Oscar and I were on our own at one point and we were able to chat casually. I didn't know if any, "trekker's etiquette" existed in these situations and whether what I was about to do was right or wrong but I thanked Oscar for all his help, his attention, his encouragement over the past six days but in particular getting me through summit night. He was invaluable to me and I am not sure if any other guide in the party could have helped me the way he did. I reached into my pocket and pulled out, I think, US$25 and handed it to him.

'Just my way of showing my appreciation,' I said.

He seemed reluctant to take it and momentarily I thought I'd dropped a clanger in offering to him.

'It's OK, Oscar,' I said, 'this is just between you and me, take it, I can't show my gratitude any other way.'

After a short while he accepted it and grinned. 'Thank you, John, my brother,' he said and we shook hands. I felt so touched. I did feel I gained a brother.

Eventually, we arrived at Mweka Gate, not the first to arrive but certainly not the last. I went for a much-needed sit down under cover from the sun whilst Oscar joined his fellow guides and porters.

Some of us, not just in our party but in all other parties attempting to conquer the mountain may see it as a romantic brave endeavour, or whatever. Many people have tried, some failed but people do it for their own particular individual reasons. On the other hand, for local people, it is a commercial enterprise. At Mweka Gate there were a number of people selling all sorts of items, souvenirs, clothing, footwear and the like. Adrian and I both spotted t-shirts that took our fancy. JUST DONE IT KILI 5895 m across the front appealed to us both so, even without haggling we bought one each. Let the world know what we'd done, why not? We had, I would add, seen similar traders at Machame Gate when we started the climb and again both of us acquired "Kilimanjaro" hats. A little naff but hey we are only going to be here once and it was our chance to help the local economy.

I was sitting under shade chatting and having a drink when I was aware that just outside was Oscar along with my newfound friend, his name escapes me, who had come in search of his boots, just as I'd asked him to. I signalled to them I'd be there shortly and removed the boots exchanging them for my trainers. I went outside and handed them over. He held them, almost hugged them and then once again offered his hand. We shook and without a word he was off again.

Having Lunch

Oscar just said, 'Thank you, John, I'll see you later, brother,' and disappeared after him.

Eventually, we boarded our bus for the trip back to Moshi. Instead of going to the hotel we were taken to a local outdoor restaurant/club for lunch. More alcohol and real food and the chance to relax properly. We sat around in the sun, drinking much needed beer in a great atmosphere. The food served was delicious I remember but exactly what it was escapes me. During lunch we were each handed an official certificate confirming we had indeed successfully summited Mount Kilimanjaro, at least those of us who had done it. I am sure it must be painful for those who hadn't completed the climb. After lunch we were to head back to the hotel on the bus but a few of us decided to walk the 15 minutes or so. Along the way we met a number of school children dressed in their blue and white uniforms. They were happy to stop and chat for a few minutes but clearly, they had seen trekkers like us before, probably many times and didn't seem that impressed.

A long drop

On arrival at the hotel, we collected our luggage that we'd left there prior to the climb and headed to our allocated rooms for a much-needed shower.

Adrian went first as I unpacked fresh clothes, then it was my turn. How good was that hot water on my weary body? So very refreshing and soothing I just stood there motionless letting the hot water run over my face and down my body. Washing myself, I was aware that black lava dust had engrained itself into my face, fingernails, toenails and anywhere else you care to imagine. I finished, dried off, leaving black streaks on the towel. Never mind, I'll shower again later. Dressing into non-trekking clothes was a delight with shorts, t-Shirt and flip-flops being the order of the day. Now, we were going on a little trip into the town centre of Moshi.

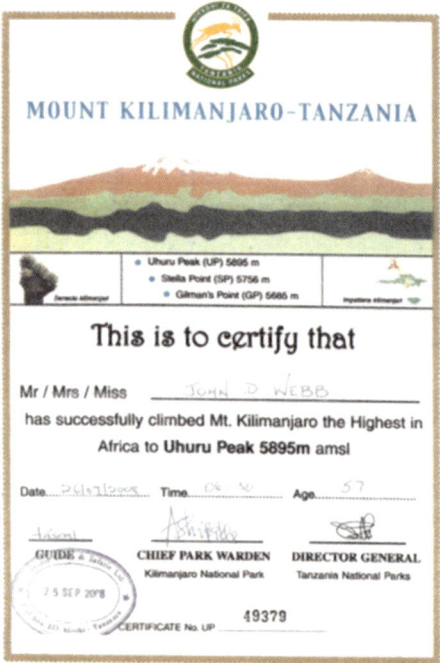

Proof I did it

Before we left, I said to Adrian to go on ahead as I wanted to make one last try to contact Susan as I knew she would be due to leave home to catch her flight to the Seychelles. To my amazement it rang. A harassed voice appeared on the other end of the telephone.

'Hiya sweetheart, it's me, aaaaahhhhgggg...' loud screams of delight were all I could hear followed by 'It's John, it's John' to her friend Eileen who was taking her to the airport.

I heard her reply. 'Well, I gathered that!'

Susan explained she was literally just about to walk out the door, another 60 seconds I'd have missed her. Fate intervened obviously. I just wanted to re-assure her I was OK and that she had a safe trip to the Seychelles and I'd see her there on Sunday.

'Bye.'

That was that. I think Susan was happy that I was able to make contact, at last, I was glad I had decided to try one final time I think she felt better having heard me directly and knew that I was in decent shape. I didn't bother to tell her that I had been struggling to breathe.

We piled onto the coach with strict instructions to be back at a certain time. On arrival a few of us stuck together wandering around and came upon an indoor/outdoor market. Now this kind of place fascinates me. Massive sacks of rice, pulses, fruit and so many other things were on display, some of which I'd never seen before and we got chatting to a one or two people. The atmosphere was fun, friendly, busy and enthralling, I could have spent all day there. We met a couple of our guides too one of whom suggested we go and see the butcher. We wandered further down the market and one guy saw us coming and immediately thrust a cockerel into our arms. A live cockerel! I'm not sure what he expected us to do with it but then it became clear that he was giving us the opportunity to have our photographs taken with the cockerel and him. I wasn't sure if this was a moneymaking stunt but he didn't ask for anything, in fairness, and was happy just to pose with a big grin on his face. Behind him was, clearly, the butcher. Not what we would call a conventional butcher in white overall but this guy was in shorts and t-shirt covered over by a kind of oilskin apron and wellington boots. In one hand he had a vicious looking long handled axe and in the other, a part of an animal carcass. His chopping block was an old tree stump and he went at his chopping with gusto and enthusiasm. The guy with the cockerel pointed out that the butcher was on drugs! That was enough, the thought of the "mad butcher of Moshi" on drugs with a vicious-looking axe made us, without a word, run like hell in all directions, much to the amusement of the guy with the cockerel. I felt sorry for the cockerel too. His fate was probably already sealed.

I went outside the market building where many other small stallholders were displaying their wares, be it household equipment such as buckets and mops or fruit which seemed to be in abundance. I turned around and saw, sitting close to one of these fruit stalls, the most strikingly, beautiful young lady that one can imagine. She caught my eye and clearly was shy but I was struck by her stunning beauty. Her very dark ebony skin shining in the sunlight, her features which to me seemed perfect and her slender body made her, I'm sure in the right place, perfect for a fashion model. I took out my camera and as she looked at me, I signalled that I wanted to take her photograph.

She just looked at me, without rebuking me or turning away, which I saw as a sign that it was OK so I took just one photograph. Within a minute I was approached by a younger female who was screaming at me like a wailing banshee. 'You pay money for taking photograph,' she shouted. 'What do you mean?' I asked.

'You take photograph so you pay money or I get police.'

'Oh for goodness sake,' I said calmly, it's only one photograph.'

'I get police, I get police' was all she could shout loudly attracting unwanted attention. I showed her the photograph on my camera and pressed delete.

'There,' I said, 'it's gone now so the police have nothing to see.'

She mumbled something and disappeared just as quickly as she had appeared. In hindsight maybe I should have given her a couple of US$ but I don't bow to attempted intimidation even from a young female but I must confess I did feel guilty afterwards

I wandered off down the road and spotted Adrian, who was looking for me. I told him what had happened. I think he was sorry he missed it.

We wandered into what was basically a souvenir shop "I Curio" turned out to be a lot more than just a basic souvenir shop. It was stocked with so many things it was clearly a sophisticated emporium. We were having a nose around and I was looking to see if there was anything, in particular, I thought just might appeal to Susan as a keepsake. As I was browsing, I absentmindedly started singing quietly "Every Step of the Way" to myself. Thinking back, I have no idea why I did sing but it must have been a natural occurrence.

There were one or two other people in the shop as well as Adrian and I just carried on perusing and singing. I found a couple of items I thought Susan might like so picked them up and took them to the counter where a lady stood, looking radiant in her bright coloured dress sporting a big smile. She was probably in her 40s and pretty. She greeted me warmly. She was, as it transpired, the Owner of the shop along with her husband and she handed me her business card.

'Great shop you have here,' I remarked, for which she thanked me.

I handed over the gifts that I had selected and she added them up. The exact amount escapes me but then she surprised me by saying, 'And 10% discount for your beautiful singing.' I was taken aback. Apart from not realising anybody could hear me, the last thing I'd call my singing is beautiful.

'Oh,' I said, 'that is so very kind.'

'You bring nice music to my shop, you get discount.' I was flattered.

Adrian and I wandered out with our thanks and goodbyes and found ourselves a coffee shop where a couple of our fellow trekkers had stopped. We all sat together chatting and laughing along with the waitress and staff. Lovely atmosphere!

I am not stupid enough to think all of Tanzania was like this but I was finding that Moshi was a really nice place to be. It is hard to describe the atmosphere but it was relaxed and people generally had smiles on their faces. I was warming to this place.

I asked Adrian if he'd had any thoughts about how he was going to transport his certificate home without creasing it or bending it and he admitted he hadn't. So, I had a brainwave.

We left the coffee shop and wandered back to the market. I spotted a guy who had an outside stall and was selling rolls of different fabrics, so approached him.

'Hi,' I said, 'do you by any chance have an old cardboard roll from the centre of your fabric that you don't want as I need to transport something back to UK with it getting bent, please?'

He knew exactly what I was after. He disappeared for a minute and came back with, indeed, a used heavy cardboard roll, about four metres long! I was looking for around about 30 centimetres. I explained this to him and straightaway he said 'No problem' and disappeared again, returning with what seemed to be a woodcutter's ripsaw.

It must have been at least 70 centimetres long with a blade so coarse it was probably good for cutting down trees. He grabbed the tube and was unable to find anywhere to rest it as he cut, so he marched out into the street and "borrowed" somebody's car bonnet as a makeshift sawhorse and proceeded to cut to the length I indicated. Hard work as the teeth were ripping the cardboard to pieces but eventually, he managed it.

'More?' he asked.

'Yes please,' I replied, 'another two just in case.' He was happy to oblige. One for Adrian and a spare just in case I thought. Having completed the task and leaving the car bonnet covered in cardboard debris, I thanked him and handed over some US$ for which he thanked me as though I'd given him the crown jewels. Of course, in a crowded street, when anything unusual happens like this, particularly when tourists are involved, it attracts onlookers. Not for the first time on this trip was I feeling as though I was the centre of attention. We left rapidly.

We met back at the coach and headed for the hotel. Tonight, we would be having a final dinner plus one or two speeches, short I hoped, then back to the club we had been at lunchtime for dancing and drinking, laughter and fun.

We convened in the hotel restaurant where we had aperitifs and chatted. Music played in the background. I had an idea. I went back to our room and grabbed a copy of Every Step of the Way and went back to the restaurant and persuaded the organisers to put it on the CD player. As it played one or two people asked who it was singing and they were pointed in my direction. Generally, it was met with approval to the point where a few of my fellow trekkers asked if they could get a copy of it. I got their addresses and promised to send a copy.

'But please,' I asked, 'add £5 to your sponsorship to pay for it rather than sending me the money. It's all going to the same place anyway.'

After a rather delicious buffet dinner we sat down to listen to a few speeches. The representative from the Alzheimer's Society, then the organiser in Tanzania, followed by George the leading UK guide. Entertaining speeches but with a serious side too, reminding us that the sponsorship money we had raised would be put to good use in helping research into Alzheimer's and hopefully, in the longer term, help future generations. At the end, George announced there were a couple of awards to give out. The first one was for, I think, the most organised trekker. A nice ripple of applause. That ruled me out then. The second was for something else notable but for the life of me I cannot remember what it was, I just wanted to go to the club. A further round of applause. Then in complete surprise George announced the final award was going to someone who had shown real guts and determination throughout the whole of the week.

'This award is going to John.'

'What?' I uttered maybe I missed it but where there two John's on this trip?

'Come on, John,' George said, 'this is for you.'

I was in disbelief I must confess and slowly approached George across the restaurant. In fairness there was a good round of applause and cheering as I accepted the award. 'Thank you' was all I could mutter and returned to my seat. The award was an oil painting of Mount Kilimanjaro in the background, a herd of cattle and a tree in the foreground with two Maasai warriors tending the cattle. It was fantastic, not just the painting but the fact that I had been deemed by my peers to have shown guts and determination. I was blown away. I didn't even know anybody had noticed.

As I write this, with a little glance over my shoulder I can see the now-framed picture which serves as a wonderful reminder of that never-to-be-forgotten week.

News of my successful summit had clearly been transmitted between my friends and family during the day, as I was receiving congratulatory texts from various people. Of course, it filled me with pride but I was so grateful people took time to contact me. I didn't expect that.

Now, however, it was time to party. I went to my room and deposited my picture in one of the cardboard tubes along with my certificate and we boarded the bus to go to the club.

On arrival, just a short time later I was amazed to see some of our porters, guides and cooks there most of them with beer bottles in hand and music playing loud, the party was already in full swing. Oscar and Justice were at the centre of attention head and shoulders over most of the others. They saw me and stopped dancing and thrust a beer into my hand and surrounded me.

'You got to dance, my brother,' Oscar shouted, so I did. Not normally in the habit of dancing with males, this was an exceptional circumstance and a special atmosphere was created by a happy collection of people from so many different backgrounds.

Everybody was dancing and drinking, there were others in the club, some of whom had also completed their treks and were letting off steam. I chatted to many or should I say shouted over the music and sadly the evening went all too quickly. Many were both intoxicated by alcohol and intoxicated by the atmosphere. I was happy, elated, so glad I was here but then we were reminded that we needed to leave. A couple of us wanted to walk back to the hotel along the pitch-black road but our organisers advised against it. 'You never know what's out there' was the comment. Scary stuff as we were not sure if they were referring to animals or bad people. We took the advice and waited until all of the team were safely on the coach.

In circumstances as we had been in, where people meet who are from various countries with diverse cultures, different religious beliefs and yes, contrasting skin colours, who can socialise, have fun and enjoy each-others company, I wonder why there are so many people in this world who harbour racial discrimination. It is one subject guaranteed to cause me so much anger when, particularly, white people demonstrate racial hatred towards people of colour, whether they be of African origin, Asian ancestry or a Caribbean background. How dare white people think they are any better than those people? What right have they got to chant defamatory messages during mass gatherings such as football matches and make ugly noises towards players of a different colour of skin to theirs and throwing fruits that only serve to demonstrate their own ignorant opinions? It is sickening. What makes white people, anywhere in the world, think they can treat non-white people so appallingly, at times? The slave trade was clearly a shameful period in the past and now, quite rightly, condemned by many but it exists as part of our history only, for all to see and be researched but cannot be erased, cannot be expunged from the record books but it belongs exactly where it is, in the past. We have surely moved on from those days. Today is built on the past and we have learned from it, be it good or bad, but whilst we live in a world that is far from Utopia, we must build on what we have gained from days and years gone by, not making the same mistakes if we are to give any chance to the generations yet to come. Slavery, racial discrimination and victimisation must no longer figure in our every-day lives in this modern futuristic-looking world. A future world that will need people of all colours, creeds and intelligence to face the many challenges that lie ahead. A divided world is a world that cannot survive. All people need to be a lot more tolerant of their neighbour's beliefs, practices and colour and be allies and not adversarial individuals or groups.

We see now in various parts of the world, prior to the start of sporting contests, players or contestants kneeling down as a sign that racism will not be tolerated and that as sportsmen, they are united in their beliefs.

I applaud it but also wonder what difference it has made. After all, the point of it is not only to show the world that there is no room for racism in sport but there is no room for it anywhere. Has it had any affect? Is racism reduced as a result of "taking the knee (I hate and disagree with that term, it's a pointless phrase)?" Sadly, I think not enough, if anything has actually changed.

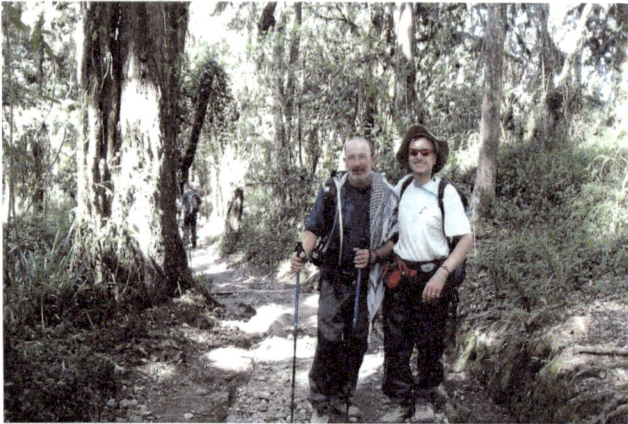

Closing in on the finish

I have travelled a lot in this world and can say I have never witnessed racism to any degree except in the United Kingdom and United States of America. In fact, as an individual I have been welcomed by people of colour in so many places be it Nigeria, Kenya, Tanzania of course, Morocco, many Countries in Europe and the Seychelles. Being warmly embraced by so many people gives an insight that proves, basically, there really is very little difference in humans anywhere in the world. I appreciate standards vary widely and that is a matter of fact but the common denominator is that we are human inside, have the same red blood, carry identical vital organs and live in this world. The only difference is, skin colour. Is that really so important? Of course, I am not naïve enough to believe all people are good people, indeed no matter what the skin colour or belief or the country, bad people exist because they are bad people for so many other reasons. The friendliness I have experienced in so many places makes me question why so much racism is prevalent in our societies. Ignorance has a lot to answer for. Maybe some of these racists should go and spend time in the homes of people who they racially abuse and learn about people whose only difference to them is skin colour. Perhaps the small minds might then be opened.

I am sure by writing this is similar to opening a can of worms but I have never had a platform on which to stand where I can say these things. Hopefully, this can be that platform and open up the debate to a wider audience and add to the voices, far more renowned than mine, that boldly take the subject directly to the racists' doorstep.

I am, of course, mindful that people have their own opinions and I am the first to agree that all people should be entitled to that, which sadly they are not when ruled by dictators and despots but is racial discrimination an opinion? Automatically I think that if, for instance, certain white people see a person of colour walking down the road, racial hatred rears its ugly head as a matter of course, just because of the skin colour. So how unreasonable is that? Do racists actually realise that the person they are abusing, whether it is outwardly or within their own minds, might just be a genuine, decent individual not looking for trouble and happy to interact with any other human and who doesn't deserve to be and has no right to be, judged by others?

Racism is certainly not confined to white people against other people of different colour. Racism exists the other way around but it seems to me not as prevalent and is not afforded the publicity that abuse by white people gets. However, no matter how much or how many times racial abuse occurs, one way or another, it is equally abhorrent and can only be condemned. I give this opinion not as a member of any organisation, brotherhood or society but as a mere individual with principles and respect for my fellow human beings.

There will always be the minority of people with extremist views in this world who are willing to undertake unspeakable and inhumane actions in the name of their beliefs, which is not necessarily colour dependent, but together, unified, the non-extremists can tolerate and persuade those who believe they are in a rank above the majority.

There is not one set of people more important than any other, whether that be based on religion, country of birth, colour or age, all are important in this world to work together, as all have a contribution to input and share in order to make the future much more harmonious not only for relatives yet to be born but for the length of time we exist on this earth in the flesh, now. What happens after that is really down to the belief, if any, of each individual but you can be sure that colour will play no part in whatever comes next.'

I swapped e-mail addresses with Oscar and Justice as we said our final goodbyes with the promise I would be in touch and send them some other Liverpool F.C. goodies. They had seen all this before, no doubt, so I figured it was standard practice for them but to me it was a goodbye like leaving good, newfound friends. In a way, sad, but from a practical point of view it was getting back to our own individual lives. They had been conducting their lives as normal for the past week, I had been taken completely out of my comfort zone into a world that I had never imagined being in just over 12 months earlier.

The bar in the hotel was closed so we were left to say our goodnight's and retire. The following day most of my travelling companions would be heading to Kilimanjaro airport to begin the journey home, two or three were going on safari on the Serengeti but I was staying an extra night in the hotel to get to the airport early Sunday morning.

Day 7

We breakfasted together in a leisurely manner. A few hangovers were obvious, and in some cases, breakfast was given a miss. Both Adrian and I were fine and we decided to take another quick trip into Moshi as departure from the hotel was around lunchtime. I remembered to pop my eight tablets today but didn't feel the need to use the inhaler. I guessed the tablets were starting to work as my breathing was somewhat easier. Basically, our female doctor didn't actually take my breath away but she certainly did help in giving it back to me.

I needed to get some cash from the hole-in-the-wall, Adrian wanted just to wander for an hour. A couple of the others wanted to come too so we shared a taxi. Killing time really!

I got my cash, I'd need some for my taxi the following day, and looked around for something else to buy but decided to wait and see what I could get duty-free on the plane to

Seychelles. The town was quite busy and we wandered around looking in shops and taking in the atmosphere. I walked along a pavement and I was fascinated to see a number of ladies sat behind a couple of rows of sewing machines working away. The others carried on walking but I stood watching how adept the ladies were using the machines. I remembered my mother using a similar old Singer sewing machine when I was a young child but these ladies were so well practised either manufacturing new items of clothing or repairing existing garments. I could have stood there much longer but became aware that time wasn't on my side so I hurried off to catch up with the others.

Pretty soon we found a taxi and headed back to the hotel where it seemed everybody was just sitting around waiting to go. One or two had started on the beer which seemed like a great idea so I joined them.

The call came for everybody to grab their gear and get it loaded onto the coach. In a way it was sad to see these people go. Having been more or less in their company for past week it would be strange to be here without those friendly faces. Still, I was going to relax in the Indian Ocean so I think I had the better option.

We said our goodbyes as the coach departed. I doubted if I'd ever see any of them again except of course for Adrian, with whom I am still in touch with today. There I was alone. Very few other guests in the hotel at this time, until of course, the next influx of trekkers would arrive later in the day. I was asked to switch rooms to smaller one, which I did, then headed for the bar. I spent a quiet hour or two reading, writing and drinking until one of the young ladies from behind the bar asked me if I liked to watch football which I told her I did.

'English football on television,' she said.

Great, I thought, *I'll go to my room and watch it.*

I paid my bar bill, thanked her and left. Switching on the TV in my room I wondered if it might be Liverpool live in the English Premier League on a Saturday afternoon in UK. Imagine my utter despair. Manchester United indeed! I switched it off and raided the mini bar.

I had arranged for a taxi to collect me at 4.00 am the following morning to get me to Kilimanjaro Airport for my flight to Nairobi, Kenya. It took about 45 minutes by taxi in the pitch black not helped by the fact that the taxi driver was the quiet type. I had to strike up conversation to ease the boredom and my questions were generally met with one-word replies. I couldn't wait to get there. I paid him my US$20 and gave him US$2 tip but I'm not sure why, that journey was hard work. I really did get the impression he didn't want to be there but taxiing is a 24-hours a day job, I couldn't feel guilty that maybe I had inconvenienced him.

I approached the airport entrance only to find one or two other people standing around. The airport wasn't yet open! Once inside, however, I was able to get a coffee and wait until the flight was called. Boarding time was 05.30 and eventually, I was on my way to Nairobi. This time, however, I was on the right side of the plane to be able to see down to Mount Kilimanjaro, in the sunlight, my last glimpse of the mountain. A few clouds were present at the summit and I imagined right then that there were other people, other trekkers, in awe of that mountain, who like me, just a few days earlier, had reached the summit at daybreak, exhausted but elated. I knew how they felt.

Chapter 5
Emotion, Resting and
Going Home

It always seems impossible until it's done.
– Nelson Mandela

Once I arrived back in Nairobi Airport, boarding for the Kenya Airways flight to Mahe Island, Seychelles was scheduled for 07.55 so I had a short time to kill. I wandered around the airport looking in the various shops but not finding anything to buy either for myself or for Susan. Nairobi airport is a typical "transit" airport. Once in the terminal building you can't go anywhere but from flight gate to flight gate. Most people arrived and then headed to another gate for their onward journey except for those actually visiting Kenya, obviously, but even at this time of the morning there were so many people scuttling around the place. I located my departure gate to make sure I knew where I was supposed to be at the allotted time, then headed off to find a coffee and managed to get a 2-day-old, British newspaper, which I proceeded to read from cover to cover as well as completing the crosswords and other puzzles. It passed the time.

I was, of course, getting excited at the thought of returning to the Seychelles and texted Susan to let her know of my progress.

'Sitting by the pool after a delightful breakfast' was her response.

Well, thanks for that, made me feel great, not!

Eventually boarding time arrived and I headed to the gate and without delay I was on the plane seated by myself and we took off on time. Plenty of room to spread out for the journey of 2,095 km (1,302 miles) and it should take about three hours.

During the journey, I was reading the newspaper and then switched to a little writing in my diary. The service from the flight crew was superb serving coffee, tea soft drinks or alcohol and also a snack for which I was grateful as I hadn't realised just how hungry I was. The one thing I noticed, however, was that the attendant serving me was always the same young lady. Beautiful face, smiling at me each time flashing her pearl white teeth in my direction. Nothing, it seemed was too much trouble.

'Thank you,' I said, 'you're very kind.'

'My pleasure,' she replied and then added, 'congratulations in climbing Mount Kilimanjaro.'

I was taken aback. How on earth did she know? Then it dawned on me. Maybe "JUST DONE IT" on my T-shirt gave it away. Idiot!

In fairness to the young lady, she did give me great attention but probably thought this old man must be tired and needs looking after, please don't have a heart attack on my plane.

I thumbed through the in-flight magazine and came upon the duty-free pages. Plenty of alcohol of course and gifts. My eyes fixed on an unusual pearl necklace. Not your ordinary creamy colour but more of a brown/bronze colour.

I attracted the attention of my newfound friend.

'Yes, we have them on board,' she said, 'I'll go and fetch them.'

Off she went returning shortly and opening the box to show me.

'Perfect,' I said and she replaced them back in the box and returned with her receipt book.

I paid her cash and she looked at me and said, 'Your wife is a lucky lady.'

'Oh, they are not for the wife,' I replied, 'they are for my girlfriend I got something else for my wife.' I laughed. Poor girl didn't know what to say. I think I embarrassed her.

Then I relieved the situation by saying, 'Only joking, they are for my wife, I hope she likes them.'

My flight attendant laughed now as she understood my joke. She looked at me as if to say, 'OK, smart arse, I got your measure.'

As we were due to come into land at Mahe, she came to check all was in order and I thanked her for all her attention and lovely personality. She seemed shy but said it was one of her more delightful trips and thanked me for being amusing, which probably meant, thanks for not having heart attack!

She warmly shook my hand as I was about to leave the aircraft and hoped I would fly Kenya Airways again. Who knows what might happen next, I thought, but I'm sure she will be just as charming, if I was on her aeroplane at some time in the future.

I went to the baggage collect area as the carousel was rolling and stood fascinated as the police search dogs scrambled over the luggage, obviously looking for drugs or any other illegal contraband, obeying their handlers, jumping over cases and bags sniffing as they went. It was an unlucky day for the dogs; they appeared to have found nothing.

I collected my bag and along with my rucksack piled them onto a trolley and meandered off to the bar. I pushed the trolley to the counter and was greeted enthusiastically by the lady standing there. It was warm and I was parched by now.

'Can I please have a Seybrew?' I asked.

'Of course, you can,' she replied, 'I'm sure you need it,' laying her eyes on my t-shirt.

I was beginning to like this shirt, it attracted beautiful ladies! Seybrew is the locally brewed Seychelles beer or lager with most of the ingredients imported from the likes of Europe, Australia and South Africa. Light in colour and cold, it is delicious and just what I needed. I had a while to kill before my 15-minute flight to Praslin Island, in fact, I had a couple of hours.

I tried to ring Susan but the phone I had was clearly crap. I did however, manage to text her again. *Frustrating to have to wait for over 2 hours to take a 15-minute flight*, I texted. *Chill the champagne.*

Champagne is on ice, hurry up.

Yeah, if I could only walk on water, I thought.

Eventually, I went to the small departure lounge for internal flights within the islands of Seychelles, checked in and went through security. No sooner had I done that when I saw my bag being loaded onto the plane. Pretty soon we were on our way in the twin-engine plane with about 20 other passengers. Out over the blue Indian Ocean and up into the sky. I was sat on the backbench seat looking straight down the plane and could see the pilot and co-pilot and on through the windscreen. There on the skyline was Praslin Island. It looked nearer than it was but we were headed straight for it. Can't wait to put my feet in the Indian Ocean.

We landed smoothly, sometimes it does get a little bumpy on landing but this time was fine, and I was first-off the plane as the door is at the rear. The baggage followed a short time later and I grabbed mine, slung my rucksack over my shoulder and wandered off to find a taxi. I knew where to go and felt confident I'd have no trouble getting a cab easily.

As I walked out of the building I was approached by a man. Now, this wasn't just any man. This was the Seychellois equivalent to Goliath. Tall, broad shoulders, I mean very broad shoulders and made me look like a 100kg weakling.

'You're going to the Acajou!' he boomed.

I was taken aback. 'Er, yes I am,' I replied mildly.

I swear if he'd said I was going to The Black Parrot or any other hotel on Praslin Island I'd have agreed to go with him. He looked and sounded terrifying.

He took my suitcase and rucksack from me.

'Follow me,' he ordered.

He opened the boot of his car, deposited my baggage in there, slammed it shut then opened the door for me to get in. I almost felt as though I was being kidnapped.

Off we set. He started laughing.

'I told your wife I'd get you, told her I'd bring you to her.'

I visibly relaxed. He explained that when Susan had arrived, he had picked her up and she told him that I'd be joining her on Sunday. He agreed to pick me up although

Susan had her doubts it would happen. Anyway, he was true to his word and we arrived at Acajou. He unloaded my luggage as Susan appeared and he saw her.

'I told you I'd bring him, didn't I,' he shouted. 'Yes,' she replied, 'thank you.'

I paid him and off he went.

Susan rushed down the stairs to me, hugging and kissing me.

'Well done, Sweetheart, I'm so proud of you,' she said.

'Thank you.' I smiled.

'Get a grip, John, you've lost weight,' she added. 'Have I?' I replied, 'I hadn't noticed.'

We were invited into the hotel lounge to be served a cocktail, which was the normal welcome for guests but, to be honest, all I wanted to do was get to our room and unpack. Eventually, we did go to our room, Number 32, our favourite. Susan opened the door and I went in noticing my baggage had already been delivered by the Hotel Porter. I looked up. The room was decorated with "well-done signs" on the patio windows and another card Susan made specially. She also handed me a parcel. I opened it to see a white t-shirt with blue writing on it saying, 'I climbed to the top of Kilimanjaro.' She explained that she had been to a shop that printed t-shirts but only wanted it when she knew I'd been successful and reached the top. From the time she knew I'd done it until she was due to leave for the Seychelles was very limited but the lady in the shop kindly agreed to print it as a matter of urgency, under the circumstances. Susan also had a shirt made for herself that said, 'He climbed to the top of Kilimanjaro.'

I sat on the bed and opened the envelope containing a card. 'You did it,' it said on the front, with a cut-out bottle of champagne and glass alongside a cut-out guy in red and yellow with the initials SJ on his shirt. SJ, to most who know me, is my nickname shortened. Ever since I was a child, I had called myself Super John or SJ for short and it had still carried on into my so-called adulthood. Inside, more cutout champagne bottles with the words lovingly written. 'CONGRATULATIONS, LET'S CELEBRATE. Well done my darling, I'm so proud of you, "My hero yet again", With all my love now and always. Susan X.' I felt the tears well up in my eyes. *Control yourself, man*, I thought, yet again. 'Thank you,' I said, 'it's wonderful. It means so much.' I placed it beside the bed.

There was only one thing I wanted to do now, before cracking open the bottle of champagne, and that was to swim in the Indian Ocean, before it got dark. I stripped and changed into my swimming shorts and we headed to the beach literally 50 metres from our room. Throwing my towel onto a sun lounger, kicking off my flip-flops I headed into the water like a kid on holiday. Oh, it was so nice. Soft white sand beneath my feet, I dived under the small waves feeling that warm water envelop me. Surfacing I flipped over onto my back and looked toward the shore where Susan stood watching.

This was real relaxation. I floated around and swam a little then headed back to the beach.

'Wow,' I said, 'that is amazing, now I know why we came here. I am so lucky to be able to do this.'

I dried off and we headed back to our room and to imbibe in our bottle of champagne. I had, I must confess, been waiting for this. Champagne is without doubt my drink of choice and for many years whenever I might do anything of note, whenever there is a birthday, bank holiday, celebration, or any other excuse it's always the champagne that comes out. I must have been a "Champagneophile", if such people exist, in my previous life.

We sat on the balcony overlooking the beach and ocean as darkness started to fall. We spoke little as we sipped our delightful, bubbly drinks, with Susan periodically asking me if I was alright. Partly exhaustion and partly emotion washed over me. Then without warning I burst into tears and sobbed my heart out. Susan stretched over to hold my arm reassuringly but it did nothing to console me. I had to let it all out, clearly.

'Stop being an emotional stupid old man,' I told myself, 'get a grip.'

Wiping my eyes, I went to the bathroom and washed my face and, taking a deep breath, returned to the balcony with my apologies.

'No need to apologise, sweetheart, I understand,' Susan said.

I just smiled. I don't think she really could but I knew what she meant.

I drank my drink and looked across at Susan.

'Time, I think, to shower, change and go and eat,' I suggested with a renewed grin on my face. 'I'm famished.'

'Good idea,' she agreed.

'OK first things first,' I said, 'did you bring a nail brush?'

Susan looked at me perplexed.

'Why on earth would I bring a nail brush?' she responded.

'I have half of Kilimanjaro embedded in various parts of my body that only a nail brush will remove,' I pointed out.

She inspected my fingernails, toenails, and eyes.

'Oh yes,' she conceded, 'part of Tanzania is now in the Seychelles.'

We laughed. I took my fourth shower since I was last on the mountain and tried as hard as I could to remove the black grime. I did, after some hard work, look a little more presentable so I changed and we headed off for dinner.

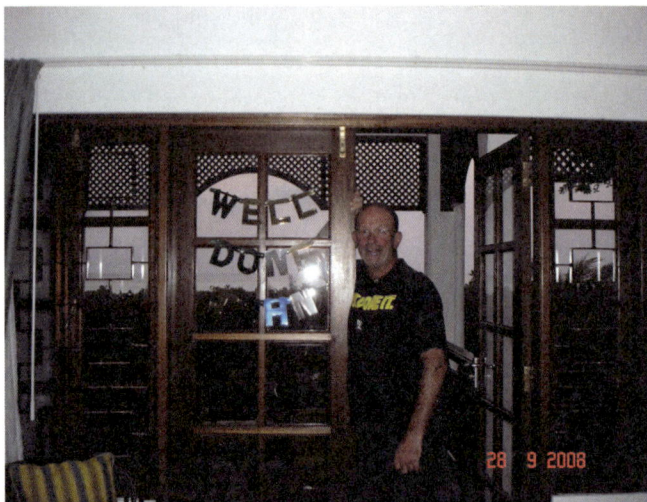

A welcome in The Seychelles

Susan went ahead of me, up the steps into the bar/lounge attached to the restaurant. There behind the bar was Betina, a young lady with whom I had previously had some good laughs and I know she was looking forward to seeing me as I was her. I hid from her view while Susan approached the bar.

'Sorry, Betina, he's not coming he decided to go back to UK instead' is all I heard.

'Oh' was the disappointing response. Susan ordered herself a drink.

Without warning I jumped into the bar from behind a plant near the door much to Betina's amazement. 'Surprise,' I shouted laughing.

Betina left what she was doing and ran around from behind the bar and hugged me, laughing too.

'Susan said you weren't coming,' she said.

'Just playing a trick on you,' I said, as I kissed her on both cheeks.

It really was lovely to see her again. Francis, the bar and restaurant Manager also appeared and shook me enthusiastically by the hand.

'Good to see you again, Mr John,' he said.

'And you, Francis,' I replied.

We stood at the bar and, sipping our G&Ts and when we could, chatted to Betina and one or two of the other staff working that night. Joanise then appeared and obviously it was great to see her again as we hugged and kissed cheeks.

She congratulated me, of course, but had to excuse herself as there were some urgent matters to attend to but we would see her throughout the week along with her delightful daughters, Manuela and Alyssa.

The meal, as I recall, was delicious. One of the things about Acajou, among the many brilliant things, is the food. Until I visited the Seychelles, I had never tasted genuine Creole food. Fish, shellfish, Chicken and curries are prominent as well as rice and different spicy sauces as well as plantains or bananas, red beans and jambalaya.

At home, cooking is my big hobby. Well more than just a hobby as Susan has only cooked a maximum of four meals in the 20+ years we have been together so it is my vocation. This, more than likely, has to be the major contributing factor to my longevity, so far. However, always willing to try new things I introduced Creole food into our diet with confidence enough to have a Creole evening five-course meal with eight other guests. It must have been alright, as everybody woke up the following morning and, as I understand, nobody had any ill effects either.

The rest of the week was one of relaxing, swimming, walking, eating, drinking and reading, writing and, of course chatting. The problem with chatting, particularly alone with Susan, was that I found it so emotional all of the time. In fact, not just when chatting I know, for instance, we would each be reading and Susan looked up to see me, on more than one occasion, with tears streaming down my face. These emotions are something I'd never experienced in my life, never so strong, never so powerful, and certainly not this uncontrollable. I kept having to tell myself to stop, but that didn't make the slightest bit of difference. Without warning I'd be blubbing as certain things entered my head.

During the week I gave Betina an "Every Step of the Way" wristband which she put on and wore with pride. A few days later she wasn't wearing it and I asked why?

'I had to take it off,' she explained, 'the colours, green and white, is a political statement in the Seychelles.'

I understood, of course, and totally respected that decision.

I had, as I previously mentioned, come up with an idea for another song. During my quiet non-blubbing moments, I had been working on this song which I had already decided was to be entitled "We Went Down". When I told Susan, her immediate reaction was, 'You do know what that can also

152

mean, don't you?' Of course, I did but my mind isn't always in the gutter, unlike some.

Anyway, "We Went Down", it was going to be but I didn't imagine for a minute it would see the light of day even after I completed it. It was a form of therapy, just writing it, I think. I managed to complete the lyrics while in the Seychelles, in the back of the diary that is now lost!

As the week wore on, I became more and more calm, nowhere near as tearful as I had been but I knew it wouldn't take much to start me off again. All too soon the week was over and we said our fond farewells to our friends at, what we had called our second home. We were on our way back to our first home, reluctantly.

In hindsight, I was so glad we had made the decision to take a week out and relax. I cannot imagine just what I would have been like had I returned home from Kilimanjaro on that Sunday, met up with Susan, she would have gone to work on Monday morning and I would have been left alone, no doubt still full of emotion but alone not able to share those feelings and thoughts with anybody else. I imagine I would have been a wreck, or drunk every day until I got it out of my system. Now en-route home, I was refreshed, clear headed and focused on my remaining duties to fulfil my commitment of collecting remaining sponsorship monies for the society.

Arriving at Heathrow Airport, London we scooted through passport control collected our baggage and passed through customs and into the arrivals hall. I marched on towards the exit and heard Susan call out to me from behind. I turned. She was stood next to a gentleman who had said something to her and she beckoned me to come back. The gentleman turned out to be from Tanzania and had read my t-shirt "I Climbed to the Top of Kilimanjaro". And Susan's "He climbed to the top of Kilimanjaro".

'I just wanted to say well done for climbing that big mountain in my country,' he said, 'and I'd like to shake your hand.'

He held out his hand which I took and shook vigorously, delighted to do so but slightly embarrassed that I had walked past him and so apologised for not seeing him. He was warm and friendly, said it was no problem and we said our goodbyes.

We were met by Susan's friend, Aileen who had been so supportive in many ways not just of my fundraising but to Susan too. She drove us home.

On entering the village, I noticed the signpost was obliterated by a white sheet with writing on it.

'Oh,' I said, 'must be somebody's birthday.'

As we got closer, I could clearly read it. Aileen slowed the car. "WELCOME BACK!" it said, with a rough drawn map of a matchstick man standing at the top of Kilimanjaro and JOHN WEBB written above it. I was overwhelmed and thrilled. *Me?* I thought, *this is for me?* Not being used to such attention quite shocked me but nevertheless I was flattered and proud. Susan and Aileen had been in on it, of course. I did briefly wonder who Susan was speaking to on the phone during our journey. Now I knew! This was the work of Andrew and his wife Suzanne.

We drove through the village. The Woodlands was busy with Sunday lunch diners, and up the hill to home. On the gate was yet another sign. "WELL-DONE JOHN", it said. I was without doubt amazed and speechless, something that doesn't happen too often.

We unloaded our luggage into the house but something appeared to be different. Everywhere I went in the house there were balloons. Balloons everywhere. In the bed, hanging from the ceiling, stuffed in lampshades, in the bath, tied to just about everything, everywhere, and even down the toilets! All congratulatory balloons! Around the house there were also banners stuck and slung all over the place. 'Welcome back,' they said and 'Well done' and 'congratulations' too. Somebody had gone to a lot of trouble to make my homecoming special and very memorable. Again, it was Andrew and Suzanne, I was informed. So kind, so thoughtful, so much fun.

Aileen had to leave us and after she'd gone, we were there, alone in the quiet. I was elated and we took a number of photographs to mark the occasion.

A number of "Well Done" cards had already arrived from family and friends and so I opened each one and read what had been written. A couple of the cards were from people I didn't really know such as Mother-in-Law's friend and a colleague of Susan but nevertheless I was appreciative of their consideration and thoughtfulness.

After that it was down to the Woodlands Tavern. We wandered down the hill on a typically village Sunday afternoon, quiet with very little traffic and nobody around.

In the Woodlands were Andrew and Suzanne just finishing their Sunday lunch. Naturally, congratulations, hugs and handshakes were given and the champagne corks popped. Not that Andrew and Suzanne could join us in a drink they were off for a week of camping so didn't want to get involved in a drinking session, understandably. Keith and Sue, owners of the Woodlands joined us in a toast and we had a pleasant, not rowdy afternoon. I was too excited to eat that could come later. For now, I was happy just to chat, drink and laugh. Truly relaxed, back home, amongst other friends

Epilogue

One day, in retrospect, the years of struggle will strike you as the most beautiful.
– Sigmund Freud

The previous year had been a struggle, there was no doubt about that. Not in a bad way but in a good way, in a beautiful way of discovery, adventure and a grown belief.

In a good way because I took on this "summons" to the mountain, really in ignorance at the start but it became better, more exciting as the year progressed. I use the word "summons" because, looking back that's what it was. Something or someone caused that poster to be where it was at that particular time then created the desire in me to want to answer that 'summons' and then saw me through the whole year. I have thought on numerous occasions how I would have felt had I not answered that "summons". Deep regret, no doubt, always wondering if I would have been successful but also never actually knowing how fantastic an experience it turned out to be. Then, in a beautiful way, because it led me to a number of places I would never have dreamed about. Not just physical places but emotional and mental places. I saw a new beauty that made my life more worthwhile, more selfless, whilst trying to raise funds to help others. Others I would never meet, never know but have a connection to, alongside those in whose memory I had done this. And a grown belief in myself as a person. The physical test I put myself through, the character that had lay dormant for many years just itching to get out for a purpose. This was it, this was that purpose. The struggle for those 12 months had followed the struggle since my dad was diagnosed with Alzheimer's, not really knowing how to best lead my life knowing, in the back of my mind, maybe, it is a genetic disease and I could succumb to it also. It dawned on me that by raising these funds I might ultimately be helping myself directly in future years. I'm really in no hurry to find out. Maybe the struggle was also finding things to tax my brain to keep me mentally active in the hope of warding off this demon.

Now I thought about it I became convinced that since Dad passed away, my life was geared up to get to this point now. To make something successful from something adverse. It was all part of the plan. Whose plan? You might well ask. Depends what you believe. I was brought up to believe in The Almighty and despite my life heading off in many irreligious directions, it is a belief I maintain to this day, so maybe it was His plan all along to stop my life from being one of those wasted. I do know that it changed me as a person. Changed my view of the world, made me much more selfless, although I will add I have always been first in the queue to help people, charity, whoever, when called upon, but this has been a sacrifice like never before, removed from my comfort zone, without force, more by desire to contribute rather than take.

I collected all my promised sponsorship money by the due date, a total sum of £6,227 which wasn't too bad I thought but in these circumstances I always want more. I was aiming for more, I wished it had been more but I was satisfied.

Within the first couple of weeks of my return I had picked up my guitar on numerous occasions in an attempt to compose music for my new song "We Went Down". It had to be a little more complex than the simple three-bar tune I had used on "Every Step of the Way" so I extended myself to a four-bar tune. I reached a point where I thought I had an acceptable melody and practised it many times. Having got to this stage I asked myself what was the point of doing this?

I decided to contact Ron at the recording studio and told him I had another song. I wasn't as enthusiastic about "We Went Down" as I had been doing "Every Step of the Way" but nevertheless Susan and I went to the studio. In fairness Ron was really interested in my trek and we sat chatting over a cup of tea before I offered up my latest composition. Going through the usual process of laying down the music first then singing the lyrics downstairs then back up while Ron worked his magic at his desk. We chatted as he worked and he was adding different sounds, making it African, as he put it. The finished product was indeed African and really sounded in keeping with the mental picture of climbing a mountain in Africa and, of course, going back down. I am not really sure what Ron's honest opinion of it was, he didn't say, but what he had produced made it sound so much better than I even had in my mind previously.

Ron turned and looked at me but I was one-step ahead of him this time.

'Yes,' I said, 'we have a second track.'

Ron was surprised, I think.

'We, and I say we, are going to do a track called "End of the Line".'

'It's appropriate,' I added.

"End of the Line" (written by Bob Dylan and George Harrison) is a song originally recorded by that wonderful supergroup, The Travelling Wilbury's. Susan and I loved the song and we'd sung it at home many times on our microphones while I accompanied on guitar but invariably, we both ended up in fits of laughter and we hardly ever completed it. We knew the words off by heart but this time we'd use a backing track to make it sound a little authentic and hopefully cut out the giggling that normally accompanied our attempts to sing it.

Ron downloaded the backing track and we were away. I went down to the microphone first and recorded my three versions of it followed by Susan who, clearly, was a little nervous not having experienced standing in front of a microphone in headphones, basically cut off from the outside world with the backing track blasting in her ears and singing the whole song, again, three times.

She reappeared upstairs and once again Ron got to work mixing the singing with the instrumentals. He added our two voices together in some places, mine in solo as well as Susan in solo too. The outcome, after a couple hours, was really good, it sounded half-decent with backing singers on the track and whilst nowhere near as polished as the professionals it was acceptable. Ron gave me the master and a copy and we headed to the car, playing it loud on the way home.

As I had with "Every Step of the Way", I made copies of it and designed a sleeve for each CD. I wonder who I could sell these to now. Friends listened, politely, and in truth most had no hesitation in buying a copy so the CD shot up to number two in my mental music charts. "Every Step" was still my number one. Sales were decent enough so I had a little more money to send to The Alzheimer's Society.

Susan's mum, Marie, rang one day, out of the blue. 'How would you like to come and give a talk about climbing Kilimanjaro to the Mothers Union group I attend?' she asked.

'I'd love to, Ma,' I replied, 'I'll need a couple of weeks to prepare it but yes definitely.'

'It will be in the church hall,' she added.

'OK, Ma, no problem.'

I started straight away by writing down the outline of what I was going to say then thought if I just stand there telling them what I'd done I can imagine one or two of the poor ladies being so bored they'd probably nod off. What I needed was something just a little bit more dynamic.

It came in a blinding flash. First of all, a flip-chart with large photographs, to accompany me talking about what I did and showing where I was and the scenery on the mountain, and in between breaking it up by singing both my songs. Seems like a plan.

I bought a large flip-chart and went through the very many photographs that I had on my computer. I had been very fortunate that quite a few of my fellow trekkers had emailed me pictures they had taken and along with my own I had ended up with over 2,000. I sifted through these and finally settled on 35 which I thought would tell the story. I arranged these on the pages of the flip-chart in order and titled each picture, then wrote the text of my talk. It would last a little over 30 minutes which I thought was long enough to keep people's attention.

I bought some wood and constructed myself an easel on which to display the chart. With that I was ready to make my debut as a public speaker. We had agreed a date and time and, slightly nervous, I turned up at the venue. I was delighted to see that quite a number of ladies had decided to attend probably just out of curiosity.

The talk started off with an introduction as to why I did the climb and before I started on the bones of it, I sang "Every Step of the Way". It seemed to go down OK. Further explanations followed along with me turning the pages of the chart revealing the photographs. I think they all got the story but just before the end I picked up my guitar again and sang "We Went Down", again it seemed to be acceptable, or were they just being polite when there was a ripple of applause? I finished off with a thank you for inviting me and I will return after I have climbed my next mountain, if you'll have me.

A round of applause followed and then a cup of tea and biscuits. I chatted to one or two of the ladies and the lady secretary announced they had a little collection and handed me an amount of money which, I said, would go directly to Alzheimer's Society. There was general agreement about that.

A week or so later I had another telephone call from Mother-in-Law.

'John, the Old Age Group I belong to heard about your talk and want you to do a talk for them please.;

I laughed.

'Sure, Ma, happy to do it,' I said.

'It's in the Scout Hall in Ystrad Mynach,' she added. 'Just let me know when,' I said.

So, that was that. I'd use basically the same material and same format so it would be easy to prepare this time.

The day arrived and I turned up as arranged. There were, perhaps, 20 ladies there. I set myself up and off I went again. Everything was going great and the ladies showed a lot of interest. I got to the point where I played "We Went Down", and off I went. For no reason whatsoever, my mouth, fingers and guitar decided to do things differently at the same time. I stopped singing, my fingers played all the wrong notes and the guitar felt like a lead weight in my arms.

I carried on manfully then shouted, 'I made a mistake,' and struggled to get myself back on track and back in the rhythm of the song, remembering in which order the words should come out. How embarrassing!

'We didn't notice,' shouted one of the ladies for which I was glad but then I thought oh that's how bad this must be when nobody noticed a mistake from the real thing!

I think at that point I decided my public speaking and singing careers were already over.

Nevertheless, the ladies were very complimentary and a couple were interested in the pieces of Pumice and Obsidian I'd brought along to display. I explained their significance. Once again, a small donation was offered by the ladies which I confirmed would go directly to the benefit of Alzheimer's.

I was in possession of some money from these donations and the sales of a few CDs and had a thought. Having sent my main donations into the society and having had a confirmation certificate I thought I'd change tack slightly and donate the money not to the national group in London where it is swallowed up in administration costs and research income but to the local branch of the society, where I knew it would be used to help give direct care to local people. It wasn't much, a little less than £100, but I sent it and received a delightful letter of thanks from the local chairperson. I felt good about doing that.

I wrote to Liverpool Football Club enclosing a photograph of Oscar and Justice wearing their newly acquired LFC shirts and explained this was halfway up Mount Kilimanjaro. Sadly, they never acknowledged it. I also wrote to Carlsberg, shirt sponsors of the club, and was delighted to receive a congratulatory letter in reply along with a Carlsberg tie, which I still have. Very thoughtful!

So, basically that was that. All the loose ends were tidied up, my kit carefully stashed away in my attic and I breathed a sigh of relief, on one hand. On the other hand, what was I to do now?

I stayed in touch with Oscar and Justice by e-mail and, in fact, I had a surprise telephone call from them too. They were doing well and I asked for their home addresses so I could send some things to them. By 31 December I had a parcel of things like a couple of Liverpool scarves, another shirt for one of the other guides, a CD of Liverpool songs including "You'll Never Walk Alone" which we had sung with gusto half way up Kilimanjaro plus a couple of photographs of us together and copies of my CDs "Every Step of the Way" and "We Went Down". Another guide, Pasqual, asked if I could send him a Manchester United scarf but I couldn't bring myself to buy one to tell the truth. Real football supporters will understand that! They received their gifts with enthusiasm and sent me e-mails of thanks, which I was pleased about. Sadly, contact was not maintained and in truth, nor did I expect it to but while I was in touch with them it was fun and if I helped them in any way then I was more than happy.

I had mentioned to Susan that if I was successful in doing this climb maybe I should continue and look at a couple of other extreme challenges. I remember she rolled her eyes but didn't deter me.

'Mount Elbrus is the highest point on geographical Europe,' I said.

'Where is that?' she inquired.

'Russia,' I replied, 'in the Caucasus Mountain Range and one of the seven summits.'

'The seven summits of what,' she asked.

'The generally accepted highest summit on each continent,' I replied. 'The actual seven can vary but usually they are, Everest (Asia), Kilimanjaro (Africa), Denali (USA), Elbrus (Europe), Vinson (Antarctica), Aconcagua (South America), Kosciuszko (Australia). Some people add an eighth which is Jaya Peak in Oceania.'

'If I complete one,' I'd said, 'maybe I could do another or two.'

Susan queried me, 'Which two?'

'Elbrus and Aconcagua,' I said.

'Then again if I was successful in doing those, I'd be a fool not to try Everest.'

'Not Everest,' she shot back, 'I'll burn your boots if you try that.'

So here I was now trying to decide what to do next and that conversation came to mind.

'You do remember I said to you ages ago that I wouldn't mind doing another mountain if I completed Kili, don't you?' I asked.

'Yes,' she said.

'Well, I've been looking at Elbrus and the climbing season is May to September. I have enough time to prepare, I am fit and I'll stay fit, so what do you think?'

I could tell by her body language, the tone of her voice she wasn't too impressed. So eased the tension by saying, 'We'll think about it, shall we?'

Not long after this fate would take a deciding hand in my future plans.

I was keeping fit enough going out two or three times a week often uphill walking and also back to Pen-y-Fan in Brecon but something wasn't right. My back was stiffening up and was feeling uncomfortable even when resting and walking was becoming more and more painful. I still went walking but didn't enjoy it as much as I had been and I was noticeably slower due to the pain. My friend Keith and I were going walking at 7.00 am twice a week but for me it was becoming uncomfortable. We even went to a local field to kick a football around and it was, at times excruciating. I'd have to lie on a wooden bench for a few minutes to rest it before I could carry on kicking the football around.

Eventually I decided to make an appointment to see the doctor who referred me to a Specialist. As before, x-rays and scans were undertaken with the result being I need further lumbar decompression surgery. Bang! There go all my plans for the future. My climbing career just ground to a halt there and then.

I underwent the second surgery pretty much as before but I was less enthusiastic about recovery than I had been previously, but thankfully I wasn't visited by the bout of depression this time during recovery as I had been after my first surgery. However, to this day I have never reached the level of fitness that I had been, certainly not enough to contemplate scaling one of the seven summits that's for sure. I guess age is somewhat against me now but writing this has given me a renewed enthusiasm I must admit. As it stands, climbing and trekking are now behind me and all I am left with is to contemplate what I had done. Brilliant memories nobody, except, ironically, for Alzheimer's disease itself, can ever take away from me.

It is no good trying to imagine what might have been as it has become irrelevant but I just carry the disappointment that I might have tried more extreme challenges, each of which would have been to raise more money, hopefully, to make it a bigger goal to attain, something to aim for that would help others and help me. Maybe the truth is that I actually started climbing far too late in life. Had I been younger, who knows where I might have ended up but apart from other things, cigarettes got in the way of that. They fed me with the desire to do nothing but generated ennui, I'm convinced. We all make mistakes in life, taking up that habit was one of my biggest.

I had achieved what I set out to achieve not just in climbing but in fund raising also and I am more than happy about that. Sadly, unknown to me at the time, Kilimanjaro became my Everest, my Aconcagua, my Elbrus.

I am not and never have been a Bear Grylls or Ranulph Fiennes type of individual, both of whom I admire greatly, but wish I had been more like them. The difficulties, the pain, the suffering, the rewards, the difference one hopes it makes are all reasons to have been able to continue raising funds and making my life worthwhile.

Having written this book about my climb of Mount Kilimanjaro and all the different elements that have contributed to it I feel it would be remiss of me not to acknowledge the help I have received, indirectly, from The Alzheimer's Society. Knowing that I was doing the climb and writing this book with this charity in mind helped so much to achieve success and, for the most part, provided the impetus to carry on. I haven't spoken to anybody directly from The Alzheimer's Society about this book or taken advice but my own experiences with the condition has been enough for me to be able to relay it here in writing, and I hope, effectively. In recognition of this I would like to donate 10% of any profit from this book to the charity, in the hope that a small contribution can help others.